Greg Williams is a barrister at Coram Chambers, specialising in Family Finance and Family Property specialist.

His work comprises Financial Remedies; TOLATA (Trusts of Land / Cohabitation disputes); and Private Client / Chancery disputes (typically Inheritance Act 1975 claims and Contested Probate). He also accepts instructions in the Court of Protection in relation to Financial and Property Affairs.

Greg is a member of both the Family Law Bar Association and the Chancery Bar Association.

A Practical Guide to TOLATA Claims

A Practical Guide to TOLATA Claims

Greg Williams
Barrister of Lincoln's Inn
Coram Chambers, London

Law Brief Publishing

Published 2019 by Law Brief Publishing, an imprint of Law Brief Publishing Ltd
30 The Parks
Minehead
Somerset
TA24 8BT

www.lawbriefpublishing.com

Paperback: 978-1-911035-97-8

To Ingrid, Olivia and Johann.

FOREWORD

With the number of cohabiting couples ever rising, the call for Parliament to enact a bespoke property adjustment regime for those who decide to live together, but not marry or become civil partners, becomes ever more loud. Pending the day when that call is answered, and in a legal landscape where the idea of a 'common law marriage' is nothing but mirage, lawyers must resort to concepts of trusts and property law as they seek to achieve a fair and equitable distribution of assets following the break-up of period of cohabitation. In modern times, it is to the Trusts of Land and Appointment of Trustees Act 1996 ['TOLATA'] and the developing caselaw under it that Family lawyers and Chancery lawyers have turned as the basis for the court's jurisdiction in this field. With these developments of the law, and the increasing volume of such cases, the need for a 'go to' textbook on the subject could not be more clear and, in this Practical Guide to TOLATA, that need has been well and truly answered.

Greg Williams, who is an expert in the field, is to be congratulated on producing a work which is at once both clear and accessible in explaining the basic concepts, before developing them through an understanding of the two seminal cases (*Stack v Dowden* and *Jones v Kernott*) and those that have followed. As its title promises, this is a 'practical guide' with, at every turn, readers being pointed to the issues that, in practice, are of importance and may, depending on the facts, turn a case round. The final section on 'Essential Procedure' most usefully brings together key information about the Family and the Civil processes which must each be mastered for an area of law which straddles the work of the Family and the Chancery jurisdictions.

This book provides all that a practitioner will need to know on this important topic. It is written by an enthusiast who has a gift for delivering complicated material in an open and conversational style. I confidently anticipate that this Practical Guide to TOLATA will find a space on the shelf of all who practice in this field.

The Rt Hon Sir Andrew McFarlane
President of the Family Division
3rd June 2019

PREFACE

This work is intended to serve as a guide to the busy cohabitation practitioner. It comprises six chapters designed to provide an insight into the points that typically arise in TOLATA claims. The chapters aim to provide the building blocks necessary to analyse a TOLATA claim; namely a guide to the relevant terminology and the case law principles which underpin the black letter law of the Trusts of Land and Appointment of Trustees Act 1996.

This book will hopefully be of use to family and chancery practitioners alike, as well as litigants in person, arbitrators and any other person who wishes to more fully understand property law in the cohabitation context. Indeed, it is the experience of the author that TOLATA claims - or cohabitation claims as some prefer to call them – transcend the areas of traditional chancery and family law work. The author recalls only too well that in the summer of 2018, while delivering a TOLATA seminar to a group of solicitors from a variety of firms, the author asked two colleagues from the same large firm which of the two of them dealt with the TOLATA claims in their office. One was the Head of the Family Department and the other was the Head of Civil Litigation. They each simultaneously pointed to the other and said: "she does!"

The purpose of this work, therefore, is to give the busy practitioner a useful guide which they can dip in and out of as may be necessary, in order that such claims need not in the future be punted off to another department. After all, it is a stimulating and growing area of work.

All endeavours have been made such that the law set out in this book is current as at 01 March 2019.

Greg Williams
March 2019

CONTENTS

CHAPTER ONE
AN INTRODUCTION TO TOLATA

A brief history of the Act

1. The year 1997 will perhaps be remembered in history for a number of reasons. New Labour swept to power in a landslide victory rarely seen in British politics. On the other side of the world, the British Government was to cede Hong Kong to the People's Republic of China following 156 years of British rule. Diana, Princess of Wales, died. A computer, Deep Blue, beat a human, Garry Kasparov, at chess over a series of matches. Dolly the Sheep was cloned. In cinema, a blockbuster by James Cameron about a large ship sinking in the North Atlantic became the then highest grossing film of all time. And in literature, the first of what proved to be a series of novels about a young wizard named Harry Potter was published by a then relatively unknown author called J K Rowling.

2. Against that context, few of the readers of this book, let alone the public at large, will specifically recall the coming into force, on 1 January 1997, of the Trusts of Land and Appointment of Trustees Act 1996. Nevertheless, the impact of that statute, the cases which have interpreted it, and the procedure which governs it already have had – or, in many cases, one day will have – a profound effect on the lives of thousands if not millions of people in England and Wales. That is because couples in cohabiting relationships are on the rise. Fewer people in England and Wales are getting married, providing a perhaps apposite context to those who would otherwise note with satisfaction the statistical reduction in the number of divorces.

3. In 2017, there were nearly 3.3 million cohabiting couples in England and Wales, representing about a fifth of all family

units.[1] The number of cohabiting couples was the fastest growing type of family in the UK between 2004 and 2014 (up by 29.7%)[2] and all the present signs suggest that cohabitants shall continue to be so – there were 100,000 more cohabiting couples even between just 2015 and 2017[3]. Furthermore, of the 3.3 million cohabiting couples last year, 1.25 million had children. According to some, cohabiting couples now account for over *half* of all family breakdowns despite making up only a fifth of the pool of parents when compared to the approximately four fifths of couples who choose to get married.[4]

4. The law relating to these cohabiting couples in England and Wales concerns strict property rights and interests. Despite widespread public opinion to the contrary, there is no such thing as a 'common law marriage'. Consequently, on the breakdown of a cohabiting couple's relationship, the parties and their advisors will be concerned with the legal principles of trusts of land; usually and specifically what are now called constructive trusts and importantly involving something termed 'common intention'.

5. That is far removed from a precise formula setting out what to do in any given circumstance. It does not even involve a wide statute based discretionary exercise to achieve a fair outcome between separating couples, as matrimonial finance lawyers will be commonly used to.[5] All too frequently in TOLATA cases, there is a winner and a loser. Those practitioners who favour the certainty that the more technical aspects of trust principles may

---

1 https://www.ons.gov.uk/peoplepopulationandcommunity/birthsdeathsandmarriages/families/bulletins/familiesandhouseholds/2017

2 https://www.ons.gov.uk/peoplepopulationandcommunity/birthsdeathsandmarriages/families/bulletins /familiesandhouseholds/2015-01-28

3 Ibid: ONS website.

4 http://marriagefoundation.org.uk/cohabiting-parents-now-account-majority-family-breakdown/

5 Namely under the under the Matrimonial Causes Act 1973, Section 25

bring to cohabitees' cases will nevertheless acknowledge that there will be cases where objectively the outcome is not always 'fair'; and the same practitioners will be mindful that they frequently need to win on both 'law' and 'fact' to achieve a successful overall outcome. Given that many cases concern those former cohabitees who failed to reduce their common intention into writing when making investments in property, it has been said, perhaps rather gravely, that "*the tenderest exchanges of a common law courtship may assume an unforeseen significance many years later when they are brought under equity's microscope and subjected to an analysis under which many thousands of pounds of value may be liable to turn on fine questions as to whether the relevant words were spoken in earnest or in dalliance and with or without representational intent.*"[6]

6. And so, to this book. In an age where the number of cohabiting couples is growing rapidly, so too does the need to give legal advice to those whose relationships end unhappily (and even, it should be said for balance, happily). Despite the now famous remarks of Ward L.J. in the Court of Appeal in *Carlton v Goodman*[7], the anecdotal experience of the author and his colleagues in Chambers is that this area of work is on the rise. Furthermore, any prospect of reform of this area of the law appears as distant today as it has been at any point since the Law Commission's Report on *Cohabitation: The Financial Con-*

---

6 Waite J, in *Hammond v Mitchell* [1991] 1 WLR 1127, at 1139.

7 [2002] EWCA Civ 545 at para 44, where Ward L.J. memorably wrote, including by the use of capital letters, as follows:

> "*I ask in despair how often this court has to remind conveyancers that they would save their clients a great deal of later difficulty if only they would sit the purchasers down, explain the difference between a joint tenancy and a tenancy in common, ascertain what they want and then expressly declare in the conveyance or transfer how the beneficial interest is to be held because that will be conclusive and save all argument. When are conveyancers going to do this as a matter of invariable standard practice? This court has urged that time after time. Perhaps conveyancers do not read the law reports. I will try one more time: ALWAYS TRY TO AGREE ON AND THEN RECORD HOW THE BENEFICIAL INTEREST IS TO BE HELD. It is not very difficult to do.*".

sequences of Relationship Breakdown was published in 2007[8]. That report was not received with the level of political appetite for reform that many would argue this area of the law deserves. It has been largely gathering dust ever since.

7. This book is divided into the following parts. The remainder of this Chapter shall set out briefly some of the most important changes brought about by the passing into force of the Trusts of Land and Appointment of Trustees Act 1996 (hereafter called 'the Act', or 'TOLATA'). It shall also deal with some of the key concepts which one typically encounters in these sorts of case.

8. Chapter 2 shall set out the full Act in greater detail, with a limited amount of commentary, where relevant.

9. Chapter 3 shall consider the background to and the detail of the significant decisions in *Stack v Dowden*[9] and *Jones v Kernott*[10] and the ascendancy of the common intention constructive trust.

10. Chapter 4 shall consider some of the extended case law and in particular those decisions which postdate *Jones v Kernott*. It shall deal with, in particular, examples of cases where the courts have used imputation to find the quantum of the parties' beneficial shares, sole name cases, investment cases, and quasi-investment cases. It shall also look at the circumstances in which one party may attempt to buy a co-owner's interest in a jointly owned property.

11. Chapter 5 shall deal with 'taking of an account' hearings and consider the origins of this area stemming back to equitable accounting principles.

---

8 LAW COM (No 307): https://www.lawcom.gov.uk/document/cohabitation-the-financial-consequences-of-relationship-breakdown/

9 [2007] 2 AC 432

10 [2012] 1 AC 776

12. Chapter 6 shall provide an overview of the procedure which may apply in a particular case, whether that be a freestanding civil claim, or one where a TOLATA issue arises in a family law application, such as a trial of a preliminary issue concerning intervenors.

13. We return to the present Chapter and the main changes brought about by the Act. The explanatory notes published by Parliament regarding the purpose of the Act reads as follows:

> "*An Act to make new provision about trusts of land including provision phasing out the Settled Land Act 1925, abolishing the doctrine of conversion and otherwise amending the law about trusts for sale of land; to amend the law about the appointment and retirement of trustees of any trust; and for connected purposes.*"[11]

14. Section 1 of the Act, in conjunction with Sections 4 and 5, creates the (then) new concept of a 'trust of land' (as to the definition of which, see Chapter 2 of this work). The (now) old concept of a 'trust for sale' as previously found in the Law of Property Act 1925, was repealed. As will be seen later in this work, there is therefore no longer any presumption of a trust for sale, something which was duly noted in the Parliamentary debate on the second reading of the Trusts of Land and Appointment of Trustees Bill in the House of Lords. In that debate, the Government's spokesperson argued that:

> "*the trust for sale mechanism is not appropriate to the conditions of modern home ownership, which represents the majority of jointly-owned real property, since it is based on an assumption that property … is intended as an investment rather than as a home, to be bought and sold as market con-*

11 See the tab marked 'Original Print PDF' on https://www.legislation.gov.uk/ukpga/1996/47/-contents/enacted for a free digital copy of the (unamended) HMSO Act.

ditions demand, with the beneficiaries being interested in the proceeds of sale rather than the property for its own sake."[12]

15. Instead, on the coming into force of the Act, the court now considers a short checklist of factors when deciding what, if any, order to make on an application for an order for sale. These are found at Section 15 which may be seen in Chapter 2.

16. Section 2 of the Act abolished the creation of all new settlements of property under the Settled Land Act 1925[13]. It was argued in Parliament that the provisions of the Settled Land Act were unduly complex and a product of a bygone age, irrelevant to the vast majority of the current wider public.[14] Furthermore, Section 3 of the Act abolished the doctrine of conversion in all new cases, although settlements created by a Will prior to the Act coming into force were exempt. The doctrine of conversion, of course, was the rule which provided that the interests of beneficiaries in land under an old trust for sale were deemed to be interests in the proceeds of sale of that land, not the land itself.

17. Sections 4 and 5 of the Act introduced trusts of land (as defined in Section 1 of the Act, above), in place of trusts for sale.

18. Sections 6 through to 9 (and the now inserted 9A) deal with the functions of trustees of land. In particular, Section 6 provides that trustees of a trust of land are to have all the powers of an absolute owner.

---

12 The quoted minister was the Government of the day's spokesperson in the House of Lords, The Lord Advocate The Lord Mackay of Drumadoon, at the Bill's second reading: https://api.parliament.uk/historic-hansard/lords/1996/mar/01/trusts-of-land-and-appointment-of

13 Although it may be possible to achieve a similar effect by a carefully drafted trust of land.

14 Ibid, see 8 above: Lord Mackay of Drumadoon's same speech.

19. Sections 10 and 11 deal with the need for consent by trustees from beneficiaries when carrying out any function under a trust of land. In the case of Section 10, that section deals with dispositions (i.e. deeds) that require trustees to obtain consent before exercising a function, and the Act limits the number of trustees who need to give such consent in favour of a purchaser to two trustees. As to Section 11, that broader section requires trustees exercising any function relating to the land to consult, so far as is practicable, the beneficiaries of full age and – insofar as is consistent with the general interest of the trust – to give effect to the majority view. However, as we shall see, Section 14 gives the court the power to override this consent if it is satisfied that it is appropriate to do so.

20. Sections 12 and 13 concern the rights of beneficiaries to occupy trust land, and it is those sections that the reader will need to familiarise herself with when considering occupation rent issues, which are dealt with in this work at Chapter 5.

21. Section 14 puts into legislative form the right for a trustee or a beneficiary to apply for an order in relation to the trust of land. This may be for an order for sale, or for any other order relating to the trust property, such as a taking of an account, or an occupation rent. It should be noted in particular that it is by this section that claimants who *seek to establish* a formal beneficial share may also apply. So, in a sole name case, where the former cohabiting partner of the legal title owner alleges that they have a share under a constructive trust, that person would bring their claim under Section 14.

22. Section 15 sets out the factors to which the court shall have regard when determining applications under Section 14. For more detail on this, see Chapter 2.

23. Section 16 concerns the rights of purchasers of trust property and is unlikely to be frequently relevant to the busy practitioner

advising former co-owners about their respective beneficial interests as between each other.

24. Section 17 confirms that Section 14 applies as equally to the proceeds of sale of any trust of land as it would have done to the property in question.

25. The remaining Sections in Part II and Part III of the Act are less relevant to this work. However, some sections therein concern such matters as interpretation and commencement provisions under the Act and are therefore set out for completeness in Chapter 2.

Some fundamental concepts and terminology

26. It is convenient at this point to examine some of the concepts which underpin the Act and the case law which interprets it.

Joint tenants

27. To start with, what is the difference between a joint tenancy and a tenancy in common? Joint tenants have equal rights to the *whole* property, and if one of them were to die, the whole property would automatically pass by the rules of survivorship to the co-owning joint tenant or tenants. A tenancy in common, however, sees the beneficial co-owners owning specified – sometimes different – shares of the property. The main practical difference between tenants in common in equal shares and joint tenants is that the property doesn't automatically pass to a co-owning tenant in common on the death of the other as the right of survivorship does not apply. On the death of a tenant in common that person's share will fall into their estate rather than pass to their co-owner.

28. In order for there to be a joint tenancy, the so-called 'four unities' of a joint tenancy must be present. They are the unities

of (1) possession, (2) interest, (3) title and (4) time.[15] The unity of possession means that each co-owner has an equal right to occupy or hold the whole of the property, as set out above. Although the courts now have statutory powers to regulate and exclude a co-owner from the property[16], at common law no such power existed. Secondly, the unity of interest means that each co-owner's interest must be identical and should arise from the same purchase or disposition. Thirdly, there must be unity of title. The co-ownership must arise from the same document, namely a completed contract for sale followed these days by registration of those interests. Fourthly, there must be unity of time. The co-owners' interests must arise at the same time. One can see how on any straightforward purchase by two co-owners, provided they specify that they wish to hold as joint tenants, the unities of time and title will plainly be met.

29. Each of these four unities must be present in order for there to be a joint tenancy. If even one of them is broken (including later on, such as by a notice of severance of joint interest), then the joint tenancy will fail and will be a tenancy in common.

30. The position with joint tenants and tenancies in common is best demonstrated with a series of examples. Take, for example, four people who desire to own property together: Mrs White, Mrs Peacock, Colonel Mustard and Professor Plum. In the first example, let us suppose they wish to hold the property as joint tenants. Using the example below, they all jointly own the whole property, in undivided shares, and they all have all the rights of an absolute owner of the property. It is not possible to quantify their respective shares individually, because they each own all of the whole jointly.

---

15 *Mikeover Ltd v Brady* [1989] 3 All ER 618.

16 TOLATA Section 13, and the Family Law Act 1996, Part IV.

Fig. 1(a) – Joint tenants

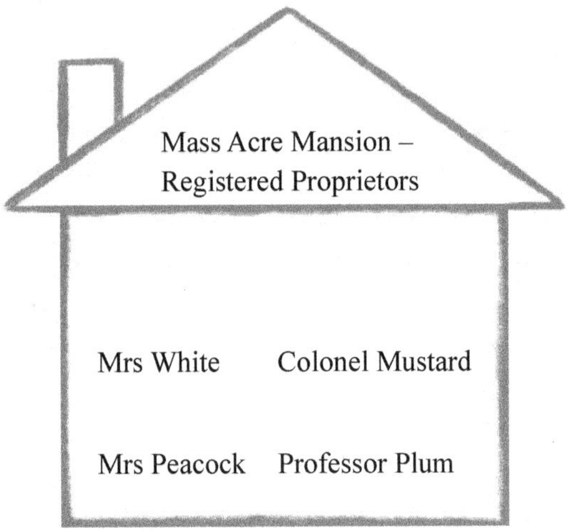

31. Suppose Mrs White were to die in tragic circumstances, leaving her three surviving friends as co-owners. The position would be that the remaining three parties would continue to own the whole property as joint tenants. Thus it would look something like this:

Fig. 1(b) – Joint tenants

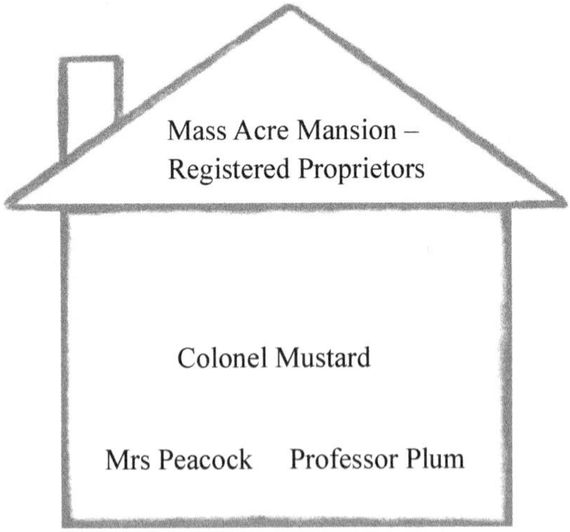

32. Then suppose Professor Plum then met an untimely death shortly after Mrs White, leaving a perhaps now worried Colonel Mustard and Mrs Peacock looking over their respective shoulders. The position would be thus:

Fig. 1(c) – Joint tenants

33. And then suppose Mrs Peacock was hit by the proverbial bus, leaving just Colonel Mustard as the sole survivor. The position would be this:

Fig. 1(d) – Joint tenants

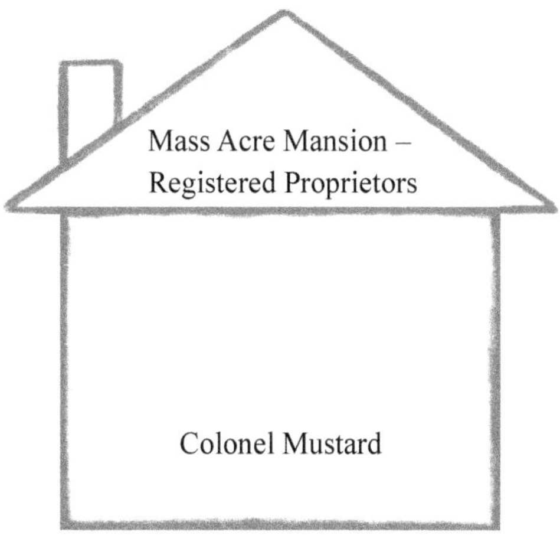

34. The reader will hopefully appreciate that with the death of each of his co-owners, Colonel Mustard has inherited one by one, by right of survivorship, the respective shares of each of his former colleagues. Following the deaths in turn of the other three, he now remains as the sole owner of the title to the property; he obviously continues to own the whole of it and continues to have the rights of the absolute owner, albeit that he no longer shares those rights with anybody else. The joint tenancy (which is, in fact, a trust of land) came to an end on the death of the last co-owner (Mrs Peacock), and Colonel Mustard is now the 100% owner (as, in theoretical terms, he always has been). He just no longer shares his ownership with any other party.

Tenants in Common

35. Let us take a second example. In this example, each of the four previously mentioned persons decided, when they bought the property, that they would not buy the property as joint tenants. (Perhaps they had a strange premonition that their co-ownership would be short.) So, instead, they decide to buy it as tenants in common in equal shares. The following diagram is illustrative of the position.

Fig 2 – Tenants in Common

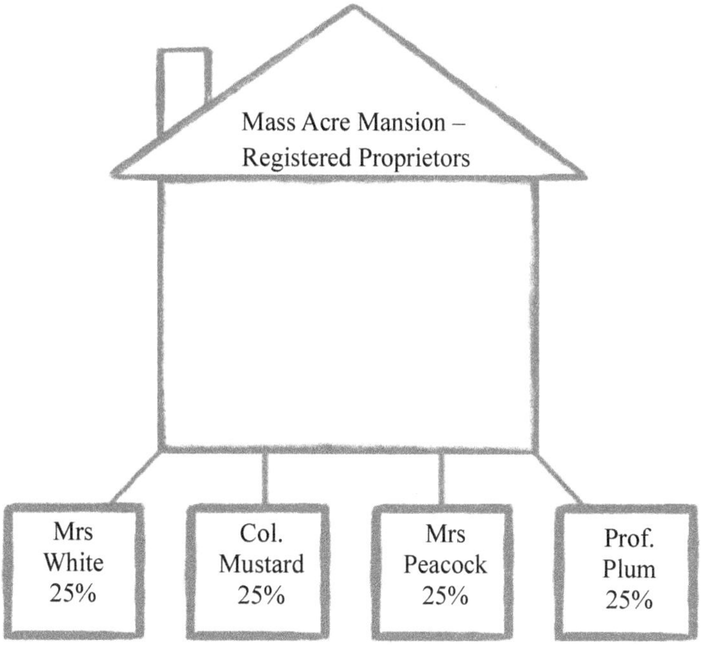

36. As tenants in common, each of the parties hold their own separate and distinct individual share. If any of the above parties were to pass away, by virtue of them being tenants in common, each person's self-contained 25% share would not automatically pass to the other legal co-owners. Instead, each party's share on death would fall into that party's estate, meaning that it could be passed on by a Will, or in the absence of a Will, under the provision of the intestacy rules.[17]

<u>Co-trustees and co-beneficiaries</u>

37. This leads to another point. When we talk about trustees and beneficiaries, we are frequently talking about parties who are both of these things at the same time. Take this example. Two parties, Jack and Jill, are in a familial relationship and they purchase a property as joint tenants in law and in equity. By that,

17 See the Administration of Estates Act 1925, Section 46, as amended.

we mean that they have purchased the legal title to the property jointly, so the outside observer would be able to see that the title to the property is registered in their names at HM Land Registry. They would also be – in this example – joint beneficial tenants (because this is a joint tenancy example), and so we would call them joint tenants in law and in equity. Jack and Jill are, in effect, co-trustees, holding the land on trust for themselves as beneficiaries under a joint tenancy. They are therefore both trustees and beneficiaries at the same time.

38. Take a second example. This time Jack and Jill decide instead to buy a property together as tenants in common in unequal shares of 60% to Jill and 40% to Jack. Again, they purchase the legal title jointly and they are registered as co-proprietors at the Land Registry. They hold the *legal* title to the property under a joint tenancy. However, because they have elected for a *beneficial tenancy in common*, the Land Registry will enter a Form A restriction (more of which, later) and the parties would be both legal trustees and equitable beneficiaries, this time holding the property on trust for themselves in the unequal shares set out above.

39. Although the purpose of this book is not to be an all-encompassing guide to conveyancing, it is worth noting that since the Law of Property Act 1925 it has been impossible for a legal estate to be held as a tenancy in common[18]. To be technical, joint owners must hold the legal estate as joint tenants, but their beneficial interests may be held either as joint tenants or as tenants in common. The reason for this in 1925 was to make conveyancing easier at a time when land registration was in its relative infancy. A purchaser of land does not need or necessarily want to know the beneficial interests of the parties who currently own the property. All a purchaser wants to be sure of is that if they are going to buy a particular property, they are taking the property free of any hidden beneficial interests. So as

18 Law of Property Act 1925, Sections 1(6) and 34.

a matter of law under the 1925 legislation, the following happens on a purchase by a third party: where there are two or more legal owners of the land (who would also be known as trustees of a trust of land under the Act), the purchaser's money, if paid to at least two of the said trustees/legal owners would be sufficient to buy out the beneficiaries' interests, whoever and whatever they might be. That process, which is called overreaching, means that the former trust of land attaches to the proceeds of sale of the land, so that the legal estate is free for the incoming purchaser to take.

40. Now take a third example – a 'sole name' case. This time Jack and Jill decide[19] to buy the property 'together' but for whatever reason the legal title is transferred into the sole name of Jill. They later separate in acrimonious circumstances and Jack says that they always intended to own the property together but in the end they purchased it for convenience in the name of just Jill. Jack says he has a beneficial share under a constructive trust and prepares to bring a court claim to establish this. In terms of the correct terminology, Jack would plead that Jill is holding the legal title to the property on trust for herself and for him. It would be up to Jack and his lawyers on the specific facts of the case to decide whether to argue that he and Jill were intended to have an equal beneficial interest or some other shareholding.[20]

19 Depending on who you later choose to believe and/or represent...

20 In a sole name case, if Jack contends and succeeds in contending that he has an equal share, it will be as a tenant in common for 50%. For Lady Hale said in *Stack v Dowden* that she knows of no instance where a sole legal owner would hold a property on a beneficial joint tenancy [paragraph 66].

What are the maximum number of legal and/or beneficial owners?

41. Under the current legislation[21], no more than four adults may hold the legal title to a property. Children may not hold legal title at all. So if Jack, Jill, Bill and Ben all decide to buy a property together, they could do so. But if they had a larger group of friends than the four of them, they would have to decide which four of them (or fewer) were going to serve as trustees for the rest of the group. Having decided that, they could then draw up a deed of trust to set out the basis of the beneficial shareholdings which underlie the legal title. In theory, there is no limit to the number of beneficiaries that the maximum of four legal trustees could hold the property on behalf of. In practice, however, the reader will usually be concerned with one trustee holding a property on trust for herself and her partner, or two trustees, holding for themselves as joint tenants or in some share or other if they have a tenancy in common. One might (relatively rarely) see a group of more than four friends collaborating with there being, say, six beneficiaries benefiting from a deed but only up to four of which can hold legal title on behalf of the group. One might also see a minor (or more than one minor) named in a trust deed as a beneficiary, but one would never see a minor as the legal title owner since as aforesaid the Law of Property Act 1925 precludes a minor from owning the legal estate.

Are express declarations of trust binding?

42. Yes. *Goodman v Gallant*[22] is good authority for the proposition that an express declaration of trust (for example, in a conveyance) is conclusive as to the demonstration of the parties' intentions of how to hold the property. The parties will be held to it, unless a successful claim is made to rescind or rectify the

---

21 S.34 Trustee Act 1925 (as amended by S.25 and Schedule 3 of TOLATA 1996).

22 [1986] Fam. 106 (Court of Appeal).

trust declaration. In that case, a married couple owned a property in the husband's sole name, although it was commonly accepted that the wife was to have a beneficial share. When the marriage broke down the husband left the property. Some years later, the wife's new partner, who had by that time started to cohabit with the wife at the property, sought to purchase the departed husband's interest jointly with the wife. When the purchase of the husband's interest was negotiated, the conveyance was specified to be into the wife and her partner's joint names. The transfer document specified that they would hold the property "upon trust to sell ... until sale upon trust for themselves as joint tenants." Later, when the wife's relationship with her partner also broke down, she severed the joint tenancy and attempted to claim that she had a greater share than her partner to the tune of 75% to 25%. She failed. The Court of Appeal gave a decisive judgment[23] and held as a general proposition that an express declaration of trust is generally conclusive. In Mrs Goodman's case, the starting point, as the Court of Appeal noted with approval citing Halsbury's Laws of England, was that "*until severance, each has the whole, but upon severance each has an aliquot part (a half or less) according to the number of joint tenants*".

43. If a party wishes to challenge an express declaration, they can only legitimately do so by way of a claim for rectification or rescission of the declaration (for example on grounds of common mistake, or fraud), and that will generally be a difficult thing to do. It is worth noting that in *Stack v Dowden* Lady Hale referred to *Goodman v Gallant* with approval. It is also worth noting that such is the simple and conclusive authority of *Goodman v Gallant*, very few TOLATA cases where there is an

---

23 One which was admirable, given that the authorities hitherto had been far from consistent. The Court of Appeal felt bound and therefore followed the following authorities: *Wilson v. Wilson* [1963] 1 W.L.R. 1470, *Leake v. Bruzzi* [1974] 1 W.L.R. 1528 and *Pink v. Lawrence*, 36 P. & C.R. 98; but note the (now disapproved) line of authority that did exist on this point only in *Bedson v. Bedson* [1965] 2 Q.B. 666 per Lord Denning M.R.

express declaration of trust will ever litigate, because unless one of the parties can prove that there was a common mistake, a fraud, or some other vitiating factor that would give rise to a claim for rectification or rescission, it is simply not worth pursuing.[24] Instead, the majority of contentious joint names TOLATA cases concern those where there was no express declaration of trust in the conveyance and therefore there is a legitimate doubt as to how the parties intended to hold the property when they purchased it. As we shall see however, since *Stack v Dowden*[25] the presumption is that equity follows the law and so even joint names cases are diminishing because Lady Hale observed it will only be in rare cases where this presumption will likely be rebutted.

24 Note however the curious decision of MacDonald J., shortly before publication of this work, in *Her Royal Highness Tessy Princess of Luxembourg, Princess of Nassau and Princess of Bourbon-Parma v His Royal Highness Louis Xavier Marie Guillaume Prince of Luxembourg, Prince of Nassau and Prince of Bourbon-Parma and another* [2018] EWFC 77 where the Court, in matrimonial finance proceedings where computation was in dispute, held that notwithstanding an express declaration of trust, the evidence before the court demonstrated that the husband did not own a beneficial share in a contentious property in the proceedings. The learned judge's reasoning, notwithstanding that he was "*acutely aware*" of *Goodman v Gallant*, was that in order for the TR1 form to be effective as a declaration of an express trust, the parties to it had to be "*able*" to declare that they would take the beneficial interest in it, Section 53(1)(b) of the Law of Property Act considered literally (and, it would appear, narrowly). In that case, the court held that at the time of the TR1 being executed, the respondent HRH The Prince of Luxembourg, was not so able because the beneficial interest in the property was already vested in the second respondent, *The L'Administration Des Biens De S.A.R. Le Grand Duc De Luxembourg*, under a resulting trust, because that party had provided the purchase monies. See in particular paras 65-67; 70; and 110 – 112.

25 [2007] 2 AC 432, House of Lords

Where should I look for an express declaration of trust?

44. Since 1 April 1997, there is a box in the Transfer of Property Form produced by HM Land Registry (known as the TR1 form). The Box can be found at Box 10 on the second page of the form. It gives joint purchasers three options for declaration: (1) to hold the property on trust for themselves as joint tenants; or (2) to hold the property on trust for themselves as tenants in common in equal shares; or (3) to hold the property on trust for themselves as tenants in common in some other share, and a space exists for the percentages to be written into the Form. A fully completed TR1 form constitutes an express declaration of trust following the rule in *Goodman v Gallant.*[26] It forms the basis of good (and arguably essential) conveyancing practice[27]. Absent a vitiating factor and a successful claim for rectification or rescission, it is seen as conclusive.

If a joint tenancy is severed, will the parties be automatically granted equal shares as tenants in common?

45. Yes. That is the effect of the rule of *Goodman v Gallant* and a number of other authorities.

46. However, there is an argument to be made, expressed as obiter in *Goodman v Gallant,*[28] that it is *possible* to provide in a deed of

---

26 But note the case of HRH Tessy *Princess of Luxembourg v HRH Louis Xavier Marie Guillaume Prince of Luxembourg, and another* [2018] EWFC 77, Ibid.

27 It never ceases to amaze the author how many cases cross his desk where a conveyance is executed without Box 10 of the TR1 Form having been completed. In some cases, such as where a conveyancer has not advised the parties to do so or set out clearly the potential effect of the various options, there may be the potential to claim for professional negligence against that conveyancer.

28 [1986] Fam. 106: See the last two pages of the reported case (starting at page 118), per Slade L.J, where his Lordship said: "*But often there is, as here, no such declaration. In such a case it used to be thought that the shares*

trust for joint purchasers to purchase under a joint tenancy, but that *in the event* the joint tenancy is severed in the future, the shares may be apportioned in something other than equal shares at that time. It should be stressed that this is not the default position, and it is only conceivable where a trust deed or other instrument has expressly provided for the same. Even then it may be open to considerable argument because these comments in *Goodman v Gallant* were, first of all, obiter and not part of the ratio decidendi, and secondly, would not appear to fit easily with the unity of interest (one of the four unities of a joint tenancy, referred to above).

<u>How can a joint tenancy be severed?</u>

47. A joint tenancy can be severed by a triggering event or act, by mutual agreement, or it can be severed unilaterally.[29] Homicide or (less drastically) the merger of interests will also serve to terminate a joint tenancy.

48. To be clear, when we talk about severing the joint tenancy we are talking about the beneficial joint tenancy.[30] In terms of a unilateral severance – which the practitioner will probably come

---

would always be equal shares.... We respectfully agree with Lord Denning M.R.'s observation, at p. 398, that "a conveyance into joint names does not necessarily mean equal shares," for it does not necessarily have this meaning when the conveyance contains no declaration of the beneficial interests: see, for example, <u>Crisp v. Mullings</u> (1975) 239 E.G. 119. He then concluded on page 119: *"It would no doubt be possible for a trust in terms to provide that the beneficial interests of two parties should be equivalent to those of joint tenants unless and until severance occurred, but that in the event of severance their interests should be otherwise than in equal shares."* On the contrary side of the argument, however, are Lady Hale's observations in *Stack v Dowden*, at para 63.

29 See *Williams v Hensman (1861) 1 J & Hem 546.*

30 Because, since the Law of Property Act 1925, it has not been possible to sever the legal joint tenancy, only the beneficial joint tenancy, see Section 36(2).

across most frequently, such as when a party positions herself to protect an interest from an ex-partner – this can be achieved by one of several ways. First, it may be express, for example, by a written notice pursuant to S.36(2) of the Law of Property Act 1925, for which precedent examples are widely available. Secondly, it may be severed by conduct, namely a 'course of dealing' provided that course of dealing is communicated to and is not done behind the back of the other party.[31] It has been held that a course of dealing does not actually require an end product before a joint tenancy is severed. For example, in *Burgess v Rawnsley* [1975] 1 Ch 429, the Court of Appeal held that aborted negotiations for a sale could amount to a course of dealings, even though they might not have resulted in a binding contract for sale.[32] Furthermore, in *Chadda and others v HMRC* [2014] UKFTT 1061, the First Tier Tribunal (Tax Chamber) accepted that a joint tenancy had been severed because without a severance, the tax planning arrangement of a husband and wife would have been ineffective. The burden of proof is on he who asserts that the joint tenancy has been severed.[33] A petition for divorce and the issuing of Form A for a financial remedy shall not automatically be sufficient to sever a joint tenancy, since a prayer for relief for a property adjustment order which may or may not be granted at some later point is not a stipulation for severance with immediate effect. However, in *Re Draper's Conveyance* [1969] 1 Ch. 486, a summons for an order for sale together with an affidavit in support affirming an intention to claim a fixed half share of the proceeds of sale was

31 Hence why it is widely accepted that a severance of a joint tenancy cannot be affected by a Will, e.g. in *Carr v Isard* [2006] EWHC 2095 (Ch); but note the case of *Perkins v Borden* [2002] WTLR 595 where a severance by Will was permitted because the evidence in that case was that the parties saw the same solicitor and had their wills drawn up together.

32 The Court also held in the same case that a joint tenancy can survive the putting of a property on the market with the intention to divide the prospective proceeds. It will be a question of fact from case to case as to whether the mutual conduct was sufficient to sever the tenancy.

33 *Greenfield v Greenfield* (1979) P&CR 570

held sufficient to sever a joint tenancy. It is therefore a question of degree.[34]

49. A joint tenancy may also be severed by a triggering event or act, such as the bankruptcy of one of the parties, or a charging order being obtained against one of the two joint tenants.[35] In the latter case, the charge will rest against the debtor tenant's sole share on severance.

What is a Form A restriction and how do you spot one?

50. A Form A restriction is a restrictive notice entered on the title register at HM Land Registry which indicates either (1) that the legal owners of the property hold the property as tenants in common rather than as joint tenants; or (2), where there is only one owner, that that owner is holding the property on trust for a beneficiary or beneficiaries. It has a tell-tale form, as follows:

> *"No disposition by a sole proprietor of the registered estate (except a trust corporation) under which capital money arises is to be registered unless authorised by an order of the court."*[36]

51. According to the Land Registry Practice Guidance notes, the purpose of a Form A restriction is to ensure that the provisions of section 27(2) of the Law of Property Act 1925[37] are complied with. That section (as amended) provides as follows:

> *"Notwithstanding anything to the contrary in the instrument (if any) creating a trust of land or in any trust affecting the*

34 *Harris v Goddard* (1983) 3 All ER 242

35 *C Putnam and Sons v Taylor and another* [2009] EWHC 317 (Ch).

36 The name 'Form A restriction' comes from the Form A set out in Schedule 4 of the Land Registration Rules 2003.

37 As amended by the Trusts of Land and Appointment of Trustees Act 1996 (section 25(1) and Schedule 3, paragraph 4.

net proceeds of sale of the land if it is sold, the proceeds of sale or other capital money shall not be paid to or applied by the direction of fewer than two persons as trustees, except where the trustee is a trust corporation, but this subsection does not affect the right of a sole personal representative as such to give valid receipts for, or direct the application of, proceeds of sale or other capital money, nor, except where capital money arises on a transaction, render it necessary to have more than one trustee."

52. In plain English, this means that the restriction will ensure one of two things. First, if there are two or more beneficial co-owners under a tenancy in common, it shall ensure that any third-party purchaser will be notified that her purchase monies will be needed to be paid to all the co-owners. Secondly, on the death of one of the tenants in common, the property subject to the trust of land cannot be sold without further ado by the surviving tenant in common on her own – which would potentially sidestep the rights of the beneficiaries of the deceased co-owner's will, or rights under the intestacy rules. For that reason, on the death of a co-owning tenant in common, a new 'co-trustee' for the trust of land needs to be found. (Obviously under a joint tenancy there would be no such need for a Form A restriction because the right of survivorship shall apply.)

53. Remember, the purpose of a Form A restriction is to ensure that the interests behind a trust can be overreached[38] upon a conveyance. Accordingly, there may not be more than one Form A restriction.[39] That is because it is not the purpose of the Form A restriction to tell the outside world the extent and quantum of the trust of land. Its only purpose is to ensure that on the pur-

38 See above.

39 Land Registry Practice Guide 19: *https://www.gov.uk/government/publications/notices-restrictions-and-the-protection-of-third-party-interests-in-the-register/practice-guide-19-notices-restrictions-and-the-protection-of-third-party-interests-in-the-register*

chase of a trust property by a third party, the trust of land attaches to the proceeds of sale leaving the legal estate free for the incoming purchaser to take.

54. If a copy of the Land Register shows a Form A restriction against the title of a property, it is a tell-tale sign that the co-owners are not beneficial joint tenants. That will either be because: (1) when the property was purchased, the parties elected to hold the property as tenants in common by way of a trust deed registered with the Land Registry, or from 1997 onwards because they set out in the TR1 Form that they intended to hold the property as tenants in common – although post 1997 they could nevertheless choose to have a separate deed of trust in the background to their declaration in the TR1; or (2) the parties failed to enter *any* expression of their beneficial holdings in the TR1 Form, in which case the Land Registry takes the necessarily cautious view to enter a Form A restriction by default; or (3), having been joint tenants initially, one or both of the parties have elected to sever the joint tenancy, and an application has been made to enter a Form A restriction onto the register.

CHAPTER TWO
THE MECHANICS OF THE ACT

1. The Trusts of Land and Appointment of Trustees Act 1996 Act (or 'the Act' as it shall hereafter be called in this work) is a relatively short statute. Yet in its brief formation it contains several relatively far reaching powers.

2. This Chapter shall set out the statutory machinery of the Act, paying particular emphasis to the key sections for most TOLATA claims.

3. In the first instance, a demonstration of the relatively brevity of the Act is best affected by setting out a (happily) concise table of its entire contents.

The Act – A table of contents

PART I: TRUSTS OF LAND

Introductory

1. Meaning of "trust of land".

Settlements and trusts for sale as trusts of land

2. Trusts in place of settlements.

3. Abolition of doctrine of conversion.

4. Express trusts for sale as trusts of land.

5. Implied trusts for sale as trusts of land.

Functions of trustees of land

6. General powers of trustees.

7. Partition by trustees.

8. Exclusion and restriction of powers.

9. Delegation by trustees.

9A. (1) The duty of care under section 1 of the Trustee Act 2000…

Consents and consultation

10. Consents.

11. Consultation with beneficiaries.

Right of beneficiaries to occupy trust land

12. The right to occupy.

13. Exclusion and restriction of right to occupy.

Powers of court

14. Applications for order.

15. Matters relevant in determining applications.

Purchaser protection

16. Protection of purchasers.

Supplementary

17. Application of provisions to trusts of proceeds of sale.

18. Application of Part to personal representatives.

PART II: APPOINTMENT AND RETIREMENT OF TRUSTEES

19. Appointment and retirement of trustee at instance of beneficiaries.

20. Appointment of substitute for incapable trustee.

21. Supplementary.

PART III: SUPPLEMENTARY

22. Meaning of "beneficiary".

23. Other interpretation provisions.

24. Application to Crown.

25. Amendments, repeals etc.

26. Power to make consequential provision.

27. Short title, commencement and extent.

SCHEDULES

SCHEDULE 1 – PROVISIONS CONSEQUENTIAL ON SECTION 2

SCHEDULE 2 – AMENDMENTS OF STATUTORY PROVISIONS IMPOSING TRUST FOR SALE

SCHEDULE 3 – MINOR AND CONSEQUENTIAL AMENDMENTS

SCHEDULE 4 – REPEALS

4. The Act came into force on 1 January 1997.[1] There have been a few, relatively minor amendments since its inception which are highlighted where relevant.

5. One further point: The Act applies to England and Wales only.[2] If by some obscure chance you are reading a copy of this work in a bookshop north of the Scottish border, please put it back on the shelf immediately.

The Act – Key Sections for the busy TOLATA practitioner

6. The key sections for the busy TOLATA practitioner are sections 14 and 15, which relate to the court's statutory powers and the matters which are relevant when the court considers applications under the Act. In a significant number of cases sections 12 and 13 will also be of relevance, as they concern the rights of parties to occupy trust property and the exclusion and restriction of those rights, usually on terms.

7. Looked at as a whole using the above Table of Contents, it can also be seen that only Sections 1 – 18 are directly relevant to the busy 'TOLATA' practitioner, namely one who is concerned with advising clients who co-own property in a family or other (perhaps investment) context.

8. That is because Part II of the Act (Sections 19, 20 and 21) deal with the 'appointment of trustees' (hence the full name of the

---

1 By virtue of Section 27 of the Act in conjunction with S.I.1996/2974.

2 Section 27(3) of the Act.

Act and its ensuing acronym) but they are not of everyday relevance to co-ownership claims. As such, they are beyond the scope of this work. For present purposes, it shall suffice to say that Part II of the Act is not necessarily irrelevant, but it is unlikely to be of assistance to everyday cohabitation disputes. Instead, Part II deals with the appointment and retirement of trustees where a trust instrument has failed to nominate sufficient trustees. An example of this may be where a trustee of a trust loses mental capacity within the meaning the Mental Capacity Act 2005.

9. Part III of the Act (Supplementary) *is* of relevance to this work, but there is very little in that Part to be excited about. It does contain a helpful definition of the meaning of a 'beneficiary' at Section 22 and clarification of whether or not the abolition of the doctrine of conversion is retrospective or not (to which the answer is, no) in Section 25. However, for present purposes, it does not add a great deal to the busy practitioner's case preparation.

10. What therefore follows in this chapter is a complete copy of the Part of the Act which is most likely to be of regular relevant, namely Part 1, up to Section 15 thereof. Included is a short commentary on the most relevant practical parts of the Act, but please also see for further detail the introductory remarks made in Chapter 1. This chapter is not intended to be a substitute for a more detailed commentary on the statutory machinery, of which other, more suitable, works are available. This is a practical guide.

PART I: TRUSTS OF LAND

Introductory

Section 1 – Meaning of "trust of land"

(1) In this Act—

(a) "trust of land" means (subject to subsection (3)) any trust of property which consists of or includes land, and

(b) "trustees of land" means trustees of a trust of land.

(2) The reference in subsection (1)(a) to a trust—

(a) is to any description of trust (whether express, implied, resulting or constructive), including a trust for sale and a bare trust, and

(b) includes a trust created, or arising, before the commencement of this Act.

(3) The reference to land in subsection (1)(a) does not include land which (despite section 2) is settled land or which is land to which the Universities and College Estates Act 1925 applies.

11. It will be noted that a 'trust of land' means any trust of property which *consists of or includes* land, and includes any description of trust (whether express, implied, resulting or constructive), trusts for sale and bare trusts, applies to trusts created or arising before the commencement of the Act on 01 January 1997.

Settlements and trusts for sale as trusts of land

Section 2 – Trusts in place of settlements

(1) No settlement created after the commencement of this Act is a settlement for the purposes of the Settled Land Act 1925; and no settlement shall be deemed to be made under that Act after that commencement.

(2) Subsection (1) does not apply to a settlement created on the occasion of an alteration in any interest in, or of a person becoming entitled under, a settlement which—

(a) is in existence at the commencement of this Act, or

(b) derives from a settlement within paragraph (a) or this paragraph.

(3) But a settlement created as mentioned in subsection (2) is not a settlement for the purposes of the Settled Land Act 1925 if provision to the effect that it is not is made in the instrument, or any of the instruments, by which it is created.

(4) Where at any time after the commencement of this Act there is in the case of any settlement which is a settlement for the purposes of the Settled Land Act 1925 no relevant property which is, or is deemed to be, subject to the settlement, the settlement permanently ceases at that time to be a settlement for the purposes of that Act

In this subsection "relevant property" means land and personal chattels to which section 67(1) of the Settled Land Act 1925 (heirlooms) applies.

(5) No land held on charitable, ecclesiastical or public trusts shall be or be deemed to be settled land after the commencement of this Act, even if it was or was deemed to be settled land before that commencement.

(6) Schedule 1 has effect to make provision consequential on this section (including provision to impose a trust in circumstances in which, apart from this section, there would be a settlement for the purposes of the Settled Land Act 1925 (and there would not otherwise be a trust)).

12. Section 2 does what it says. It abolishes settlements for the purposes of the Settled Land Act, although it only applies to new settlements from 1 January 1997 onwards and does not have retrospective effect.

Section 3 – Abolition of doctrine of conversion

(1) Where land is held by trustees subject to a trust for sale, the land is not to be regarded as personal property; and where personal property is subject to a trust for sale in order that the trustees may acquire land, the personal property is not to be regarded as land.

(2) Subsection (1) does not apply to a trust created by a will if the testator died before the commencement of this Act.

(3) Subject to that, subsection (1) applies to a trust whether it is created, or arises, before or after that commencement.

13. The effect of this section is to abolish to doctrine of conversion, as to which, see Chapter 1 for further explanation. In short, going forward, the position is that the beneficial interests of parties shall exist in the land itself, rather than be deemed to be interests in the proceeds of sale of that land.

Section 4 – Express trusts for sale as trusts of land

(1) In the case of every trust for sale of land created by a disposition there is to be implied, despite any provision to the contrary made by the disposition, a power for the trustees to postpone sale of the land; and the trustees are not liable in any way for postponing sale of the land, in the exercise of their discretion, for an indefinite period.

(2) Subsection (1) applies to a trust whether it is created, or arises, before or after the commencement of this Act.

(3) Subsection (1) does not affect any liability incurred by trustees before that commencement.

14. As noted in Chapter 1, since 1996, there is no longer any presumption that a trust of land is a *trust for sale*, because of the

replacement of Section 30 of the Law of Property Act 1925 (which provided for the same) and the instigation of Section 4 of TOLATA, as set out above. Old trusts for sale are now *Trusts of Land.*

Section 5 – Implied trusts for sale as trusts of land

(1) Schedule 2 has effect in relation to statutory provisions which impose a trust for sale of land in certain circumstances so that in those circumstances there is instead a trust of the land (without a duty to sell).

(2) Section 1 of the Settled Land Act 1925 does not apply to land held on any trust arising by virtue of that Schedule (so that any such land is subject to a trust of land).

15. This tidies up some of the above previous sections.

Functions of trustees of land

Section 6 – General powers of trustees

(1) For the purpose of exercising their functions as trustees, the trustees of land have in relation to the land subject to the trust all the powers of an absolute owner.

(2) Where in the case of any land subject to a trust of land each of the beneficiaries interested in the land is a person of full age and capacity who is absolutely entitled to the land, the powers conferred on the trustees by subsection (1) include the power to convey the land to the beneficiaries even though they have not required the trustees to do so; and where land is conveyed by virtue of this subsection—

(a) the beneficiaries shall do whatever is necessary to secure that it vests in them, and

(b) if they fail to do so, the court may make an order requiring them to do so.

(3) The trustees of land have power to [acquire land under the power conferred by section 8 of the Trustee Act 2000].

(4) . . . (repealed)

(5) In exercising the powers conferred by this section trustees shall have regard to the rights of the beneficiaries.

(6) The powers conferred by this section shall not be exercised in contravention of, or of any order made in pursuance of, any other enactment or any rule of law or equity.

(7) The reference in subsection (6) to an order includes an order of any court or of the [Charity Commission].

(8) Where any enactment other than this section confers on trustees authority to act subject to any restriction, limitation or condition, trustees of land may not exercise the powers conferred by this section to do any act which they are prevented from doing under the other enactment by reason of the restriction, limitation or condition.

[(9) The duty of care under section 1 of the Trustee Act 2000 applies to trustees of land when exercising the powers conferred by this section.]

16. This is an important section in concept, although one rarely needs to refer to it in day-to-day TOLATA cohabitation claims. It should be noted that Section 6 provides that trustees of a trust of land are to have all the powers of an absolute owner, and indeed have the power to convey the land to the beneficiaries (whether the beneficiaries desire them to or not). In practice, this helps bare trustees (also known as nominees) to cease to act in such a capacity. It should be noted, furthermore,

that trustees have to have regard to the rights of the beneficiaries, per sub-section (5). In other words, in a TOLATA claim, a legal owner's absolute powers are curtailed by the requirement to have regards to the rights of any beneficiaries that they hold the trust property for. So, say if there were two parties holding the property jointly on trust for themselves as joint beneficiaries[3], one co-owner should not be exercising his 'absolute' rights unilaterally because (a), there is a joint trustee with whom he should have regard, and under this section (b) he or she must consider the beneficiaries (who are one and the same).

Section 7 – Partition by trustees

(1) The trustees of land may, where beneficiaries of full age are absolutely entitled in undivided shares to land subject to the trust, partition the land, or any part of it, and provide (by way of mortgage or otherwise) for the payment of any equality money.

(2) The trustees shall give effect to any such partition by conveying the partitioned land in severalty (whether or not subject to any legal mortgage created for raising equality money), either absolutely or in trust, in accordance with the rights of those beneficiaries.

(3) Before exercising their powers under subsection (2) the trustees shall obtain the consent of each of those beneficiaries.

(4) Where a share in the land is affected by an incumbrance, the trustees may either give effect to it or provide for its discharge from the property allotted to that share as they think fit.

---

3 For further explanation of this point and a series of worked examples, see Chapter 1.

(5) If a share in the land is absolutely vested in a minor, subsections (1) to (4) apply as if he were of full age, except that the trustees may act on his behalf and retain land or other property representing his share in trust for him.

[(6) Subsection (1) is subject to sections 21 (part-unit: interests) and 22 (part-unit: charging) of the Commonhold and Leasehold Reform Act 2002.]

17. This section gives the trustees (and indeed the Court) the power to partition land subject to a trust of land, although there is a requirement to obtain the consent of each of those beneficiaries before this power may be exercised.

Section 8 – Exclusion and restriction of powers

(1) Sections 6 and 7 do not apply in the case of a trust of land created by a disposition in so far as provision to the effect that they do not apply is made by the disposition.

(2) If the disposition creating such a trust makes provision requiring any consent to be obtained to the exercise of any power conferred by section 6 or 7, the power may not be exercised without that consent.

(3) Subsection (1) does not apply in the case of charitable, ecclesiastical or public trusts.

(4) Subsections (1) and (2) have effect subject to any enactment which prohibits or restricts the effect of provision of the description mentioned in them.

18. Section 8 allows for a disposition creating a trust of land to expressly omit the application of Sections 6 and 7, although that is not possible in the case of charitable, ecclesiastical or public trusts.

Section 9 – Delegation by trustees

(1) The trustees of land may, by power of attorney, delegate to any beneficiary or beneficiaries of full age and beneficially entitled to an interest in possession in land subject to the trust any of their functions as trustees which relate to the land.

(2) Where trustees purport to delegate to a person by a power of attorney under subsection (1) functions relating to any land and another person in good faith deals with him in relation to the land, he shall be presumed in favour of that other person to have been a person to whom the functions could be delegated unless that other person has knowledge at the time of the transaction that he was not such a person.

And it shall be conclusively presumed in favour of any purchaser whose interest depends on the validity of that transaction that that other person dealt in good faith and did not have such knowledge if that other person makes a statutory declaration to that effect before or within three months after the completion of the purchase.

(3) A power of attorney under subsection (1) shall be given by all the trustees jointly and (unless expressed to be irrevocable and to be given by way of security) may be revoked by any one or more of them; and such a power is revoked by the appointment as a trustee of a person other than those by whom it is given (though not by any of those persons dying or otherwise ceasing to be a trustee).

(4) Where a beneficiary to whom functions are delegated by a power of attorney under subsection (1) ceases to be a person beneficially entitled to an interest in possession in land subject to the trust—

(a) if the functions are delegated to him alone, the power is revoked,

(b) if the functions are delegated to him and to other beneficiaries to be exercised by them jointly (but not separately), the power is revoked if each of the other beneficiaries ceases to be so entitled (but otherwise functions exercisable in accordance with the power are so exercisable by the remaining beneficiary or beneficiaries), and

(c) if the functions are delegated to him and to other beneficiaries to be exercised by them separately (or either separately or jointly), the power is revoked in so far as it relates to him.

(5) A delegation under subsection (1) may be for any period or indefinite.

(6) A power of attorney under subsection (1) cannot be an enduring power of attorney or lasting power of attorney within the meaning of the Mental Capacity Act 2005.

(7) Beneficiaries to whom functions have been delegated under subsection (1) are, in relation to the exercise of the functions, in the same position as trustees (with the same duties and liabilities); but such beneficiaries shall not be regarded as trustees for any other purposes (including, in particular, the purposes of any enactment permitting the delegation of functions by trustees or imposing requirements relating to the payment of capital money).

(8) . . . (repealed)

(9) Neither this section nor the repeal by this Act of section 29 of the Law of Property Act 1925 (which is superseded by this section) affects the operation after the commencement of this Act of any delegation effected before that commencement.

[9A Duties of trustees in connection with delegation etc]

[(1) The duty of care under section 1 of the Trustee Act 2000 applies to trustees of land in deciding whether to delegate any of their functions under section 9.

(2) Subsection (3) applies if the trustees of land—

(a) delegate any of their functions under section 9, and

(b) the delegation is not irrevocable.

(3) While the delegation continues, the trustees—

(a) must keep the delegation under review,
(b) if circumstances make it appropriate to do so, must consider whether there is a need to exercise any power of intervention that they have, and

(c) if they consider that there is a need to exercise such a power, must do so.

(4) "Power of intervention" includes—

(a) a power to give directions to the beneficiary;

(b) a power to revoke the delegation.

(5) The duty of care under section 1 of the 2000 Act applies to trustees in carrying out any duty under subsection (3).

(6) A trustee of land is not liable for any act or default of the beneficiary, or beneficiaries, unless the trustee fails to comply with the duty of care in deciding to delegate any of the trustees' functions under section 9 or in carrying out any duty under subsection (3).

(7) Neither this section nor the repeal of section 9(8) by the Trustee Act 2000 affects the operation after the commencement of this section of any delegation effected before that commencement.]

[Author's note: Section 9A was not originally in the Act as passed by Parliament in 1996. It was inserted by the Trustee Act 2000, s 40(1), Sch 2, Pt II, para 47.]

19. This relatively long section (and added sub-section under the Trustee Act 2000) deals with the power of trustees to delegate by power of attorney, any of their functions as trustees which relate to the land to a beneficiary or beneficiaries of the trust of land.

Consents and consultation

Section 10 – Consents

(1) If a disposition creating a trust of land requires the consent of more than two persons to the exercise by the trustees of any function relating to the land, the consent of any two of them to the exercise of the function is sufficient in favour of a purchaser.

(2) Subsection (1) does not apply to the exercise of a function by trustees of land held on charitable, ecclesiastical or public trusts.

(3) Where at any time a person whose consent is expressed by a disposition creating a trust of land to be required to the exercise by the trustees of any function relating to the land is not of full age—

(a) his consent is not, in favour of a purchaser, required to the exercise of the function, but

(b) the trustees shall obtain the consent of a parent who has parental responsibility for him (within the meaning of the Children Act 1989) or of a guardian of his.

20. Section 10 deals with dispositions (for instance, by way of a deed) that require trustees to obtain consent before exercising a function. The Act limits the number of trustees who need to give such consent in favour of a purchaser to two trustees. This means that in circumstances where there are, say, three trustees of land, the consent of the two in the majority is all that is needed to sell the property. In cases where there may be four trustees, again, only the consent of two are needed. If the person whose consent is needed is a minor, a person with parental responsibility for that child can give good consent.

Section 11 – Consultation with beneficiaries

(1) The trustees of land shall in the exercise of any function relating to land subject to the trust—

(a) so far as practicable, consult the beneficiaries of full age and beneficially entitled to an interest in possession in the land, and

(b) so far as consistent with the general interest of the trust, give effect to the wishes of those beneficiaries, or (in case of dispute) of the majority (according to the value of their combined interests).

(2) Subsection (1) does not apply—

(a) in relation to a trust created by a disposition in so far as provision that it does not apply is made by the disposition,

(b) in relation to a trust created or arising under a will made before the commencement of this Act, or

(c) in relation to the exercise of the power mentioned in section 6(2).

(3) Subsection (1) does not apply to a trust created before the commencement of this Act by a disposition, or a trust created after that commencement by reference to such a trust, unless provision to the effect that it is to apply is made by a deed executed—

(a) in a case in which the trust was created by one person and he is of full capacity, by that person, or

(b) in a case in which the trust was created by more than one person, by such of the persons who created the trust as are alive and of full capacity.

(4) A deed executed for the purposes of subsection (3) is irrevocable.

21. Section 11 requires that trustees exercising any function relating to the land to consult, so far as is practicable, the beneficiaries of full age; and insofar as is consistent with the general interest of the trust, to give effect to the majority view. That requirement is certain unless a disposition provides to the contrary, or in relation to a will trust which arose before the Act came into force. As noted in Chapter 1, however, the court has the express power under Section 14(2)(a) to relieve trustees of the need to obtain the consent of, or consult with any beneficiary with whom they would otherwise be obliged to do so. Obviously, in TOLATA claims where two co-owners are at loggerheads, this permits the court to make an order in favour of one party, overruling the wishes of the other, the actual result of which would depend on the circumstances of the case.

22. The next sections are 12 and 13. It is worth setting them out together.

Right of beneficiaries to occupy trust land

Section 12 – The right to occupy

(1) A beneficiary who is beneficially entitled to an interest in possession in land subject to a trust of land is entitled by reason of his interest to occupy the land at any time if at that time—

(a) the purposes of the trust include making the land available for his occupation (or for the occupation of beneficiaries of a class of which he is a member or of beneficiaries in general), or

(b) the land is held by the trustees so as to be so available.

(2) Subsection (1) does not confer on a beneficiary a right to occupy land if it is either unavailable or unsuitable for occupation by him.

(3) This section is subject to section 13.

Section 13 – Exclusion and restriction of right to occupy

(1) Where two or more beneficiaries are (or apart from this subsection would be) entitled under section 12 to occupy land, the trustees of land may exclude or restrict the entitlement of any one or more (but not all) of them.

(2) Trustees may not under subsection (1)—

(a) unreasonably exclude any beneficiary's entitlement to occupy land, or

(b) restrict any such entitlement to an unreasonable extent.

(3) The trustees of land may from time to time impose reasonable conditions on any beneficiary in relation to his occupation of land by reason of his entitlement under section 12.

(4) The matters to which trustees are to have regard in exercising the powers conferred by this section include—

(a) the intentions of the person or persons (if any) who created the trust,

(b) the purposes for which the land is held, and

(c) the circumstances and wishes of each of the beneficiaries who is (or apart from any previous exercise by the trustees of those powers would be) entitled to occupy the land under section 12.

(5) The conditions which may be imposed on a beneficiary under subsection (3) include, in particular, conditions requiring him—

(a) to pay any outgoings or expenses in respect of the land, or

(b) to assume any other obligation in relation to the land or to any activity which is or is proposed to be conducted there.

(6) Where the entitlement of any beneficiary to occupy land under section 12 has been excluded or restricted, the conditions which may be imposed on any other beneficiary under subsection (3) include, in particular, conditions requiring him to —

(a) make payments by way of compensation to the beneficiary whose entitlement has been excluded or restricted, or

(b) forgo any payment or other benefit to which he would otherwise be entitled under the trust so as to benefit that beneficiary.

(7) The powers conferred on trustees by this section may not be exercised—

(a) so as prevent any person who is in occupation of land (whether or not by reason of an entitlement under section 12) from continuing to occupy the land, or7

(b) in a manner likely to result in any such person ceasing to occupy the land,

unless he consents or the court has given approval.

(8) The matters to which the court is to have regard in determining whether to give approval under subsection (7) include the matters mentioned in subsection (4)(a) to (c).

23. Sections 12 and 13 concern – and provide the Court with the power to regulate – the rights of beneficiaries to occupy trust property. Section 12(1) provides that a beneficiary entitled to an interest in possession in land subject to a trust of land may ordinarily occupy that trust property, within certain parameters such as the purpose of the trust being available for occupation of that beneficiary, or for the occupation of beneficiaries of a class of which he is a member or of beneficiaries in general. In the case of a family home, purchased in order to house two cohabiting or formerly cohabiting parties, one can immediately see the statutory underpinning contained in this section to the right to occupy. In *Stack v Dowden*[4], Lord Neuberger recognised that while the right to occupy was equitable in origin, they are now governed by Sections 12 to 15 of TOLATA. However, he noted that it would be a "rare case" where "*the statutory would produce*

4 [2007] 2 AC 432, 478; Lord Neuberger at para 150 onwards

a different result from that which would have resulted from the equitable principles."[5] Section 12 is specifically subject to Section 13.[6]

24. Section 13 sets out entitlement of trustees of trusts of land to exclude or restrict the entitlement of beneficiaries to occupy trust land. Under Section 13(1), where there are two or more beneficiaries, the trustees of land may exclude or restrict the entitlement of any one or more (but not all) of them. Bearing in mind what was said in Chapter 1 that in the cohabitee context the parties may each be both trustees and beneficiaries, either may have an argument to exclude the other – and impose conditions, and/or to be liable to pay compensation to the other – under this Section. The Court, of course, has the power to determine any such dispute as to the exercise of the trustees' powers.[7] A decision to try to exclude a beneficiary, co-beneficiary or co-trustee/beneficiary should not be made lightly. That is because a trustee operating under Section 13(1) may not unreasonably exclude any beneficiary's entitlement to occupy land[8] or restrict any such entitlement to an unreasonable extent[9] Further, when exercising their powers under this section, trustees are required to have regard to those matters set out in Section 13(4), which include the intentions of the person or persons who created the trust, the purposes for which the land is held, and the circumstances and wishes of each of the beneficiaries otherwise entitled to occupy the land.[10] The trustees may from time to time impose reasonable conditions on any beneficiary in relation to his occupation of the land. Those conditions

5 Ibid, also at para 150.

6 Section 12(3).

7 Section 14.

8 Section 13(2)(a).

9 Section 13(2)(b).

10 Similarly, if the Court is *adjudicating on a contentious dispute between the parties, it has regard to exactly the same criteria, per Section 13(8).*

may include, in particular, conditions to pay any outgoings or expenses in respect of the land, or to assume any other obligation in relation to the land or to any activity which is or is proposed to be conducted there.[11] Further, when the entitlement of any beneficiary to occupy land has been excluded or restricted, the conditions which may be imposed on any other beneficiary (perhaps he who remains in occupation to the other's detriment) may include making payments by way of compensation to the beneficiary whose entitlement has been excluded or restricted, or forgoing any payment or other benefit to which they would otherwise be entitled under the trust so as to benefit that beneficiary. Finally, the powers contained in Section 13 are not intended to provide a legal route to ouster, as Section 13(7) makes clear. In the cohabitation context, Section 13 may be used to try to regulate the position once one party has departed a property either of their own volition, or by agreement, or by separate court order. If a party requires assistance due to domestic abuse, they would be better off seeking assistance from a specialist family lawyer and availing themselves of the right to apply for a non-molestation order or an occupation order under the Family Law Act 1996, Part IV.

Powers of court

Section 14 – Applications for order

(1) Any person who is a trustee of land or has an interest in a property subject to a trust of land may make an application to the court for an order under this section.

(2) On an application for an order under this section the court may make any such order—

(a) relating to the exercise by the trustees of any of their functions (including an order relieving them of any obligation

11 Section 13(5).

to obtain the consent of, or to consult, any person in connection with the exercise of any of their functions), or

(b) declaring the nature or extent of a person's interest in property subject to the trust,

as the court thinks fit.

(3) The court may not under this section make any order as to the appointment or removal of trustees.

(4) The powers conferred on the court by this section are exercisable on an application whether it is made before or after the commencement of this Act.

25. Section 14 is the section that the busy TOLATA practitioner will return to time and time again. It permits either a trustee or a beneficiary to seek an order from the court in relation to the trust property, and provides the mechanism for doing so when another co-owner resists or opposes, because, under Section 14(2)(a) the court has the power to make an order reliving the claimant of the obligation to obtain the consent of any other connected person. Section 14 importantly grants the court the power to order declaratory relief.[12] Note that the Court does not *create* the parties' shares in the property, it merely *finds* them – and then declares what they are. This is because the case law[13] makes it abundantly clear that the search is for the parties' shared intentions, whether actual, inferred or imputed.[14] Having found them, the court can then *declare* what they are. The Court cannot redistribute the parties' shares between them in order to move towards what the court considers would provide a fairer outcome[15]. The Act contains no such redistributive

12 Section 14(2)(b).

13 See Chapters 3 and 4 of this work.

14 *Stack v Dowden* [2007] 2 AC 432 at 455, per Lady Hale, at para 60.

power[16]. Among orders capable of being made under Section 14 are orders for sale, and/or for the taking of an account – which may include a claim for occupation rent. Where a former cohabitee seeks to establish a beneficial interest in a property held in their ex-cohabitee's sole legal name, the court may determine that claim under this section, granting declaratory relief if the claimant is successful.

Section 15 – Matters relevant in determining applications

(1) The matters to which the court is to have regard in determining an application for an order under section 14 include—

(a) the intentions of the person or persons (if any) who created the trust[17],

(b) the purposes for which the property subject to the trust is held,

(c) the welfare of any minor who occupies or might reasonably be expected to occupy any land subject to the trust as his home, and

(d) the interests of any secured creditor of any beneficiary.

---

15 To do so would be unlawful and would provide the basis for a successful appeal, such as in *Capehorn v Harris* [2016] 2 FLR 1026.

16 As exists, for example, as between married couples on the breakdown of their marriage under the Matrimonial Causes Act 1973, Section 24.

17 Which has subsequently been held to have meant the parties' intentions prior to the creation of the trust, per Arden L.J. in *W v W* [2004] 2 FLR 321. Lady Justice Arden observed that "if Parliament meant the present intention, it would have used some such word as 'wishes' rather than the word 'intention' which implies some statement or opinion as to the future." But given the way that the law has developed since 2004 with both *Jones v Kernott* (2011) and *Barnes and Phillips* (2015) holding that it is possible for the parties' intentions to change, this proposition may require further exploration in cases yet to come.

(2) In the case of an application relating to the exercise in relation to any land of the powers conferred on the trustees by section 13, the matters to which the court is to have regard also include the circumstances and wishes of each of the beneficiaries who is (or apart from any previous exercise by the trustees of those powers would be) entitled to occupy the land under section 12.

(3) In the case of any other application, other than one relating to the exercise of the power mentioned in section 6(2), the matters to which the court is to have regard also include the circumstances and wishes of any beneficiaries of full age and entitled to an interest in possession in property subject to the trust or (in case of dispute) of the majority (according to the value of their combined interests).

(4) This section does not apply to an application if section 335A of the Insolvency Act 1986 (which is inserted by Schedule 3 and relates to applications by a trustee of a bankrupt) applies to it.

26. Section 15 sets out the factors to which the Court shall have regard when determining applications under Section 14. It has been held that the factors at (1) (a), (b) (c) and (d) are not exhaustive and are also not in any particular order.[18] The Court is required to have regard to the factors set out in Section 15 and take each of them into account. Each case will turn on its own facts.[19] Further, sub-section (3), namely that the court shall

---

18 *Mortgage Corporation v Shaire and others; Mortgage Corporation v Lewis Silkin (a firm) and another* [2001] Ch 743; [2000] 1 FLR 973, per Neuberger J. (as he then was). That case also makes the obiter observation that that although it would be wrong to disregard the entire wealth authority which came before the Act came into force, such authorities must now be regarded as being of limited, let alone decisive, assistance.

19 For instance, see the decision of Ward L.J. in *Woodman v Tracey* [2002] EWCA Civ 880 where, in – what must be stressed as being a fact specific case – the court did not afford greater weight to the welfare of the minor

consider and take account of "*the circumstances and wishes of any beneficiaries of full age and entitled to an interest in possession in property" (or a majority thereof) applies* to all applications other than ones under Section 13 – exclusion and restriction of a right to occupy, or Section 6(2) – the right of trustees to convey trust land to the beneficiaries.[20] In respect of applications under Section 13, the court shall further have regard to sub-section (2). It should also be noted that Section 15 does not apply to an application by a trustee in bankruptcy, where instead the (partly similar, but by no means identical) factors found in Section 335A(2) of the Insolvency Act 1986 (as amended) are to be used instead.

teenage child under (c) than it did to the rights of a secured creditor under (d).

20 See Neuberger J's judgment in *Mortgage Corporation v Shaire* at page 991 of the reported decision in the Family Law Reports [2000], Vol 1.

CHAPTER THREE
THE ASCENDANCY OF THE COMMON INTENTION CONSTRUCTIVE TRUST

An Introduction

1. The common intention constructive trust has seen its fair share of controversy. The division in the House of Lords as to the correct approach to cohabitation disputes was quite apparent upon publication of the decision in *Stack v Dowden*[1].

2. To Lady Hale, the resurgence of the constructive trust in *Oxley v Hiscock* three years earlier was a demonstration that "*the law has indeed moved on in response to changing social and economic conditions*".[2] Lady Hale noted, with approval, that academics had cheered the *Oxley v Hiscock* decision as being an "*important breakthrough*".[3] Her Ladyship also noted – and seemingly took encouragement from – the Law Commission's call for a "*holistic approach*" to quantification in its 2002 discussion paper: '*Sharing Homes*'.[4]

3. As the reader will already know, Lady Hale's speech in *Stack v Dowden* was seminal. It created a new 'maxim' for chancery and family lawyers alike: "*equity follows the law*"; and her speech achieved wide contemporaneous praise for its analysis of the changing domestic cohabitation context in England and Wales.

---

1 [2007] 2 AC 432

2 [2007] 2 AC 432 Page 455 at para 60.

3 Lady Hale's speech at paragraph 61 cites *Gray & Gray, Elements of Land Law,* 4th ed, p 931, at para 10.138.

4 Law Commission in Sharing Homes: A Discussion Paper (No. 278), November 2002, para 4.27.

4. But the constructive trust did not escape without criticism. Lord Neuberger, in the same case, called it something which "is *hard to identify, particularly in the abstract.*" His Lordship said that it may lead to "*highly fact-sensitive*" cases, which may be "*contentious... even where there is no dispute as to what was done or said.*"[5]

5. In the result, Lady Hale's view won the day. Lord Hoffman agreed with Lady Hale. So too did Lord Hope. Lord Walker also agreed with Lady Hale, delivering also what his Lordship described as an "extended footnote" judgment to her Ladyship's Speech. That footnote was proffered after Lord Walker's self-deprecatory suggestion in the opening paragraphs of his speech that he had failed to better Lady Hale's legal opinion and had therefore had to set aside as redundant most of his own opinion which he had previously prepared.[6]

6. Of course, the decision in *Stack v Dowden* answered a great number of questions, principally, of course, which species of

---

5 [2007] 2 AC 432 at 473, Paragraph 129.

6 There had been some speculation in the aftermath of that decision that Lord Walker had originally intended to agree with Lord Neuberger and find in favour of the resulting trust doctrine. The speculation goes that it was only at a relatively late stage that Lord Walker read Lady Hale's speech in draft and was so impressed by the force of it that he changed his mind. In the result, that went on to leave Lord Neuberger as the sole dissenting judge, in what was his first case as a member of the Appellate Committee of the House of Lords. Some years later, that speculation was all but confirmed – with tact and without mentioning names, of course – in a lecture given by Lord Neuberger to the Denning Society at Lincoln's Inn. Lord Neuberger: "*Judgment and Judgments - the art of forming and writing judicial decisions*", 30 November 2017, paragraph 29. The speech was delivered shortly after Lord Neuberger's retirement as President of the Supreme Court. The full text can be found via the Lincoln's Inn website at *https://www.lincolnsinn.org.uk/members/denning-society/*

implied trust[7] prevails in the domestic cohabitation context, and the starting point in joint names cases. In time, however, the decision attracted a degree of academic debate for the questions that it left seemingly unanswered, such as whether there was truly a single regime for sole and joint names cases; and in what circumstances and how may the parties' intentions be adjudged to have changed? The answers to those questions were left to be dealt with in the later appeal of *Jones v Kernott*[8], of which more later.

7. The next section provides an overview of the case law prior to *Stack v Dowden*, before going on to look at that decision in detail.

The background to the decision in Stack v Dowden

8. The case law prior to *Stack v Dowden* dates back a number of decades. However, a sufficient underpinning for the purposes of the busy practitioner may be found in two particular and well-known House of Lords authorities from the early 1970s, namely *Pettitt v Pettitt*[9] and *Gissing v Gissing*[10]. Of later importance was also to be *Lloyds Bank plc v Rosset* [1991] 1 AC 107, also covered here.

9. In *Pettitt v Pettit,* the claimant husband brought a claim under section 17 of the Married Women's Property Act 1882, seeking to be beneficially entitled to a share in the proceeds of sale of the former matrimonial home. The property in question had been

---

7 In other words, constructive or resulting trusts? The answer, of course, was constructive trusts.

8 [2012] 1 AC 776. See the joint speeches of Lady Hale and Lord Walker at paragraphs 2 and 16.

9 [1970] AC 777

10 [1971] AC 886

purchased out of the proceeds of sale of a previous house which the wife had inherited. The husband's claim was based on his having done work on the house by way of redecoration and improvement which he said had enhanced its value. The parties had spent nine years living in the wife's property. The House of Lords held that on the evidence it was not possible to infer any common intention of the partics that the husband by doing work and expending money on materials for the house should acquire any beneficial proprietary interest and the husband's claim failed. In words which are as true today as they were then, Lord Reid noted:

> *"The real difficulty is in inferring from some vague evidence of an arrangement what in fact the arrangement was."*[11]

10. In any event, Lord Reid went on to hold that the difficulty with the improvements that the husband had made was that they were nearly all of an ephemeral character. Redecoration, he said, will only last for a few years and it is unreasonable that a spouse would obtain a permanent interest in a property in return for making improvements of that character.

11. Lord Morris of Borth-y-Gest, agreeing with the result, noted that the wife owned the property when the parties went to live in it and the husband had no title to it and never thought that he had.[12] Further, it had never been suggested that there had been any subsequent agreement varying the rights of the parties. The assertion of the husband that he had acquired an interest could only be accepted if the court could impute to the parties some common intention that the husband was to acquire an interest in the property commensurate with the value of the work that he did. Lord Morris could see no justification for any such imputation, and added that he did not think that the work

11 [1970] AC 777 at 796 at B to C.

12 Ibid. at 806B

done by the husband went beyond what a reasonable husband might be expected to do anyway.

12. Lord Hodson agreed. He noted that there was no agreement (no common intention, we might say today) between the husband and the wife as to any payment to be made by former to the latter for improvements made to her property. Lord Upjohn also agreed. He held that in the absence of any agreement, and on there being no question of any estoppel, one spouse who does work or expends money upon the property of the other has no claim whatever upon the property of the other.[13]

13. *Gissing v Gissing*[14] was decided just over one year later. In that case the parties were again married. The parties had bought a property in the name of the husband and which became the parties' marital home. The husband had paid the house deposit by way of a loan obtained by his employers and by way of a mortgage in his sole name. The wife contributed a relatively small sum of money towards the costs of furnishings and the laying of a lawn. The House of Lords held that as the wife had made no contribution to the acquisition of title to the matrimonial home, it could not be inferred that the parties intended her to have any beneficial interest in it.

14. In *Gissing*, three of the Appellate Committee of the House of Lords were the same as those sitting in *Pettitt*: Lord Reid, Lord Diplock, and Lord Morris of Borth-y-Gest. Lord Morris, agreeing with the majority, made the following observations which encapsulate the issues in these cases (what we now call 'TOLATA' cases):

> *"The court does not decide how the parties might have ordered their affairs: it only finds how they did. The court*

13 Idib. 818 at E.

14 [1971] AC 886.

> *cannot devise arrangements which the parties never made. The court cannot ascribe intentions which the parties in fact never had. Nor can ownership of property be affected by the mere circumstance that harmony has been replaced by discord. Any power in the court to alter ownership must be found in statutory enactment."*[15]

15. But *Gissing* is probably most well-known because of Lord Diplock's speech. Having found himself in the minority in *Pettitt*, Lord Diplock was very much leading the majority in *Gissing*. In *Gissing*, Lord Diplock was less concerned with the taxonomy of trusts: "*A resulting, implied or constructive trust – and it is unnecessary for present purposes to distinguish between these three classes of trust – is created by a transaction between the trustee and the cestui que trust in connection with the acquisition by the trustee of a legal estate in land, whenever the trustee has so conducted himself that it would be inequitable to allow him to deny [it]*".[16] His Lordship said, rather famously, as follows:

> *"... Parties to a transaction in connection with the acquisition of land may well have formed a common intention that the beneficial interest in the land shall be vested in them jointly without having used express words to communicate this intention to one another; or their recollections of the words used may be imperfect or conflicting by the time any dispute arises. In such a case - a common one where the parties are spouses whose marriage has broken down - it may be possible to infer their common intention from their conduct.*[17]*" (with emphasis from the author)*

16. One important point of terminology here – and one which arguably led to significant interpretive difficulties in the Court

15 [1971] A.C. 886 at P 898.

16 [1971] AC 886, at P.905.

17 [1971] A.C. 886 Page 906.

of Appeal in the decades that followed – was the interchangeable use by Lord Diplock of the words "infer" and "impute" in his speeches in *Pettitt* and then in *Gissing*. As Lord Walker was to later note in *Stack v Dowden*, Lord Diplock used the word 'impute' at least eight times in the crucial part of his dissenting speech in *Pettitt*[18], but used instead the word 'infer' in Gissing at least 23 times.[19]

17. So, although in *Gissing* the wife did not come even close (on the appeal) to meeting the necessary requirements to lead to a trust arising in her favour (remember she had made only insignificant improvements to the property), Lord Diplock's speech did set a precedent about the potential to find common intention which was to dominate the law for years to come. As Lord Denning M.R. was later to comment enthusiastically in *Eves v Eves*: "*Lord Diplock brought it into the world and we have nourished it*"[20].

18. If the busy practitioner will permit this work to fast forward twenty years or so, one arrives at the decision in *Lloyds Bank plc v Rosset*[21]. This case was slightly different, because although it too concerned a husband and a wife and was a 'sole name case', here a creditor was involved. Mr and Mrs Rosset purchased the subject property as a home for themselves and their two children. They used money from the Husband's family trust, which was based in Switzerland, to purchase the property. The Swiss trustee, with both parties' knowledge, insisted on the acquisition being in the husband's sole name. However, the property required a great deal of renovation. Perhaps unconven-

18 See Lord Walker at [2007] 2 AC 432, P 443 quoting Lord Diplock at [1970] AC 777, 822h to 825e.

19 Lord Walker in Stack, ibid. at 443, summarising Lord Diplock in *Gissing v Gissing* [1971] AC 886 at 906b-910a.

20 [1975] 1 WLR 1338, 1341

21 [1991] 1 AC 107

tionally, the vendors of the property gave the defendants permission to enter the property with builders to undertake renovation work before exchange of contracts. The builders began work on the property two weeks before contracts for sale were exchanged, and the wife herself carried out decorating work almost daily, obtaining necessary materials and generally urging on the builders. Contracts were exchanged two weeks later. After that, but three days before completion of the purchase, the husband, *without* his wife's knowledge, sought and obtained permission from Lloyds Bank to overdraw up to £15,000 on his current account with them to meet the cost of the renovation. In doing so, he signed the bank's form of legal charge. Completion then took place in the husband's sole name (as originally envisaged) but in the end a proportion of the price came from the use of the husband's overdraft facility. The wife made no financial contribution either to the purchase of the property or to the cost of renovation.

19. The marriage broke down one year after the purchase. The husband left the property and the wife and children remained. The bank formally demanded repayment of the loan and when it was not met, they claimed possession and an order for sale. The husband did not resist the claim but the wife alleged by way of defence that she had a beneficial interest in the property under a constructive trust that qualified as an overriding interest under section 70(1)(*g*) of the Land Registration Act 1925 – as it then was[22] – because she had been in actual occupation of the property on the relevant date.

20. At first instance, the judge rejected the wife's claim that it had been expressly agreed between the husband and herself that the property was to be jointly owned. He found, however, that there had been a common intention between the parties formed

22 Section 70(1)(*g*) of the Land Registration Act 1925 has now been replaced with Schedules 1 (para 2) and Schedule 3 (para 2) of the Land Registration Act 2002.

prior to completion that the wife should have a beneficial interest in the property under a constructive trust and that, by virtue of the work that she had done towards the renovation of the property before that date, she had acted to her detriment on the faith of that common intention. He concluded, however, that she had not been in actual occupation of the property on that date and that, accordingly, her equitable interest as against the husband was not protected as an overriding interest by section 70(1)(*g*) of the Act of 1925 so as to prevail against the bank's legal charge.

21. The Court of Appeal, by a majority, allowed an appeal by the wife. On a second appeal by the Bank to the House of Lords, Lord Bridge noted that following another recent decision by the House in *Abbey National Building Society v. Cann*[23], the relevant date for ascertaining whether an interest in registered land was protected by actual occupation so as to prevail against the holder of a legal estate as an overriding interest under section 70(1)(*g*) of the Land Registration Act 1925 was that of the transfer or creation of the estate, not of its registration. But because of the decision that Lord Bridge was about to make about Mrs Rosset's claim for a constructive trust, it was not necessary for the House of Lords to examine whether she had been in actual occupation or not on the date of the transfer. They went on to dismiss her claim.

22. It is noteworthy that following the various – and arguably disparate – speeches in Pettitt and Gissing, this time the Appellate Committee of the House of Lords coalesced around the single judgment of Lord Bridge. Lord Bridge held that Mrs Rosset's activities in relation to the renovation of the property between the beginning of November 1982 and the date of completion, on which the judge had based his inference of a common intention that she should have a beneficial interest in it, had been insufficient to justify that inference, and, accordingly, the

23 [1991] 1 A.C. 56

trial judge's finding that the husband held the property as constructive trustee for himself and the wife could not be supported.

23. It is important to examine the material part of Lord Bridge's speech in two stages. That is because Lord Bridge's speech has a relatively short ratio decidendi, whereas his Lordship is arguably more famously remembered for his comments which were, strictly speaking, not part of the main decision and which were therefore obiter dicta. The ratio (which was approved unanimously by Lord Griffiths, Lord Ackner, Lord Oliver and Lord Jauncey), was as follows:

> *"On any view the monetary value of Mrs. Rosset's work expressed as a contribution to a property acquired at a cost exceeding £70,000 must have been so trifling as to be almost de minimis. I should myself have had considerable doubt whether Mrs. Rosset's contribution to the work of renovation was sufficient to support a claim to a constructive trust in the absence of writing to satisfy the requirements of section 51 of the Law of Property Act 1925 even if her husband's intention to make a gift to her of half or any other share in the equity of the property had been clearly established or if he had clearly represented to her that that was what he intended. But here the conversations with her husband on which Mrs. Rosset relied, all of which took place before November 1982, were incapable of lending support to the conclusion of a constructive trust in the light of the judge's finding that by that date there had been no decision that she was to have any interest in the property. The finding that the discussions "did not exclude the possibility" that she should have an interest does not seem to me to add anything of significance.*
>
> *These considerations lead me to the conclusion that the judge's finding that Mr. Rosset held the property as constructive*

trustee for himself and his wife cannot be supported and it is on this short ground that I would allow the appeal.[24]

24. But Lord Bridge did not stop there. Having allowed the appeal on that ground, he went on to make, as aforesaid, some further – and now well-known – remarks. His Lordship added, obiter:

> *"I do, however, draw attention to one critical distinction which any judge required to resolve a dispute between former partners as to the beneficial interest in the home they formerly shared should always have in the forefront of his mind.*
>
> *The first and fundamental question which must always be resolved is whether, independently of any inference to be drawn from the conduct of the parties in the course of sharing the house as their home and managing their joint affairs, there has at any time prior to acquisition, or exceptionally at some later date, been any agreement, arrangement or understanding reached between them that the property is to be shared beneficially. The finding of an agreement or arrangement to share in this sense can only, I think, be based on evidence of express discussions between the partners, however imperfectly remembered and however imprecise their terms may have been. Once a finding to this effect is made it will only be necessary for the partner asserting a claim to a beneficial interest against the partner entitled to the legal estate to show that he or she has acted to his or her detriment or significantly altered his or her position in reliance on the agreement in order to give rise to a constructive trust or a proprietary estoppel.*
>
> *In sharp contrast with this situation is the very different one where there is no evidence to support a finding of an agreement or arrangement to share, however reasonable it might have been for the parties to reach such an arrangement*

24 [1991] 1 AC 107 at P131-132

> *if they had applied their minds to the question, and where the court must rely entirely on the conduct of the parties both as the basis from which to infer a common intention to share the property beneficially and as the conduct relied on to give rise to a constructive trust. In this situation direct contributions to the purchase price by the partner who is not the legal owner, whether initially or by payment of mortgage instalments, will readily justify the inference necessary to the creation of a constructive trust. But, as I read the authorities, it is at least extremely doubtful whether anything less will do*.*[25]* (*author's emphasis)

25. As Lord Walker was to later observe in Stack v Dowden, "*... in concurring in this passage the House was unanimously, if unostentiously, agreeing that a "common intention" trust could be inferred even when there was no evidence of an actual agreement.[26]*"

26. Further, Lord Walker, when agreeing with Lady Hale in *Stack v Dowden* about the need to move the law onwards (as we shall see), respectfully doubted whether Lord Bridge's speech in *Rosset "took full account of the views (conflicting though they were) expressed in Gissing v Gissing" by* Lord Reid and Lord Diplock. In other words, his Lordship was seemingly of the opinion that the bar had been set rather too high.

27. Before we get to *Oxley v Hiscock* and *Stack v Dowden*, it is worth pausing briefly to note two other cases which were reported in the 1990s.

28. In *Springette v Defoe*[27], the Court of Appeal tried to reconcile the competing doctrines of resulting and constructive trusts in joint names cases by holding that the starting point was the resulting

25 Ibid, P.132-133

26 Stack v Dowden, [2007] 2 AC 432 P 445 at para 25

27 [1992] 2 FLR 388

trust doctrine – and specifically that the purchasers would hold the property in the proportions in which they contributed directly or indirectly to the purchase price – unless there was sufficient specific evidence of their common intention that they should be entitled in other proportions, such as equal shares; and thereby rebut the presumption of a resulting trust.[28] *Springette v Defoe* was largely disapproved by the House of Lords in *Stack v Dowden.*[29]

29. Then there was *Drake v Whipp*[30], a sole name case where both parties had made direct contributions to the purchase and the conversion of a property (a barn) in Mr Whipp's name. In that case, Mrs Drake contributed 40% of the costs of the purchase of the barn, but when one factored in the contributions which the parties made to the conversion as well, her total contribution was only 20% of the whole of the project. Thus arose the debate about whether the resulting or the constructive trust approach was to be preferred. The trial judge found that there was a common intention for the parties to hold the beneficial ownership in shares corresponding to their <u>overall</u> contributions (namely both the costs of purchase and the conversion), whereas Mrs Drake had contended that there was no common intention and that the Court should simply consider the contributions made to the purchase price (which, had she succeeded, would have ignored Mr Whipp's greater contribution to the conversion and left her with a larger share). She failed. Peter Gibson L.J. (with whom Hirst L.J. and Forbes J. agreed) held that it would "be artificial" to decide the case on resulting trust principles.[31] Indeed, as Lord Walker was to later note in *Stack v*

---

28 [1992] 2 FLR 388 per Dillon L.J. at 392, citing himself in the earlier case of *Walker v Hall* [1984] FLR 126. Lord Justice Dillon also memorably remarked in *Springette v Defoe* that "T*he court does not as yet sit, as under a palm tree, to exercise a general discretion to do what the man in the street, on a general overview of the case, might regard as fair*": [1992] 2 FLR 388 at 393.

29 [2007] 2 AC 432, at 457, para 65.

30 [1996] 1 FLR 826

31 Ibid, at P 830.

Dowden, had Mrs Drake's argument for the resulting trust been followed, it would have been "doubly artificial, as it would have unnaturally split the project into two elements, only one of which was to be taken into account in the resulting trust exercise; and it would have ignored the parties' actual common intention for the project as a whole."[32]

Oxley v Hiscock

30. The next major step on the road to *Stack v Dowden* was the significant decision of the Court of Appeal in *Oxley v Hiscock*[33]. The leading judgment in *Oxley v Hiscock* was given by Chadwick L.J., with whom both Mance L.J. (as he then was) and Scott Baker L.J. agreed.

31. *Oxley v Hiscock* was a sole name case. The claimant, Miss Oxley, who was divorced from her husband, was living in a council house with her children when she began a relationship with the defendant Mr Hiscock, who had his own house. In 1987 she exercised her right to buy her council property at the discounted price of £25,200 using funds provided by Mr Hiscock from the sale of his own property. Later, in 1991, they parties purchased a bigger property, which formed the subject of their dispute, to accommodate themselves and Miss Oxley's children. The purchase price of the second property was £127,000, and was funded by the net proceeds of sale of Miss Oxley's former council house of £61,500 (but of which £25,200 was attributable to Mr Hiscock's original contribution towards that property as opposed to £36,300 from Miss Oxley); by a further £35,500 from the Mr Hiscock's own savings; and by a mortgage loan of £30,000.

---

32 [2007] 2 AC 432 Page 446 at para 31.

33 [2005] Fam 211

32. The property was registered in the sole name of the Mr Hiscock with the consent of the Miss Oxley given despite her solicitor's advice that she should protect her interest by joint registration. After the purchase both parties contributed towards the maintenance and improvement of the property from pooled resources in the belief that each had a beneficial interest. By 2001 the mortgage had been paid off.

33. The relationship between the parties broke down, and the property was sold. Miss Oxley applied under Section 14 of the Trusts of Land and Appointment of Trustees Act 1996 for a declaration that the proceeds of sale of the property were held on trust for both parties in equal shares. The circuit judge at first instance concluded that in the absence of any express agreement, both parties had evinced an intention to share the benefit and the burden of the property jointly and equally and declared that Miss Oxley was entitled to a half share in the proceeds of sale.

34. Mr Hiscock appealed, contending that since there had been no discussion between the parties as to the extent of their respective beneficial shares at the time of purchase, the presumption of a resulting trust was not displaced and the property was held on trust for both parties in beneficial shares proportionate to their contributions (of which, of course, he had made the greater amount).

35. Enter Lord Justice Chadwick. In a highly influential judgment, which was to be extensively referenced by Lady Hale in *Stack v Dowden* three years later, Chadwick L.J. surveyed the various and contrasting Court of Appeal decisions in this area of the law since *Gissing*. His Lordship's judgment as a work of scholarship cannot be underestimated and it is commended as useful – and perhaps essential – extra reading. For present purposes, we can proceed directly to his Lordship's summary of the legal prin-

ciples, set out at paragraph 68 of the judgment onwards, and which are necessary to set out in full:

> *[68] I have referred, in the immediately preceding paragraphs, to "cases of this nature". By that, I mean cases in which the common features are:*
>
> *(i) the property is bought as a home for a couple who, although not married, intend to live together as man and wife;*
>
> *(ii) each of them makes some financial contribution to the purchase;*
>
> *(iii) the property is purchased in the sole name of one of them; and*
>
> *(iv) there is no express declaration of trust.*
>
> *In those circumstances the first question is whether there is evidence from which to infer a common intention, communicated by each to the other, that each shall have a beneficial share in the property.*
>
> *In many such cases—of which the present is an example—there will have been some discussion between the parties at the time of the purchase which provides the answer to that question. Those are cases within the first of Lord Bridge's categories in Lloyds Bank plc v Rosset [1991] 1 AC 107. In other cases—where the evidence is that the matter was not discussed at all—an affirmative answer will readily be inferred from the fact that each has made a financial contribution. Those are cases within Lord Bridge's second category. And, if the answer to the first question is that there was a common intention, communicated to each other, that each should have a beneficial share in the property, then the party who does not become the legal owner will be held to have*

acted to his or her detriment in making a financial contribution to the purchase in reliance on the common intention.

[69] In those circumstances, the second question to be answered in cases of this nature is: "what is the extent of the parties' respective beneficial interests in the property?" Again, in many such cases, the answer will be provided by evidence of what they said and did at the time of the acquisition. But, in a case where there is no evidence of any discussion between them as to the amount of the share which each was to have—and even in a case where the evidence is that there was no discussion on that point—the question still requires an answer. It must now be accepted that (at least in this court and below) the answer is that each is entitled to that share which the court considers fair having regard to the whole course of dealing between them in relation to the property. And, in that context, "the whole course of dealing between them in relation to the property" includes the arrangements which they make from time to time in order to meet the outgoings (for example, mortgage contributions, council tax and utilities, repairs, insurance and housekeeping) which have to be met if they are to live in the property as their home."**

(*author's emphasis)

36. These are important building blocks to case analysis for the TOLATA practitioner, so let us break this part of the judgment down a bit. In a sole name case, there are two questions to be answered. The 'first question' is whether there is evidence from which to infer a common intention, communicated by each to the other, that each shall have a beneficial share in the property. If there is to be an affirmative answer to that question, it is likely to fall into one of the following two 'categories': (i) those where there was an *actual discussion* at the time of purchase; or (ii) where there was no such express discussion but where an affirmative answer can still be readily be inferred from the fact that each has made a financial contribution. Taking a step back,

a discussion alone is unlikely to be enough, for two reasons. First, in *Lloyds Bank v Rosset,* Lord Bridge made the point that even a discussion or promise by the legal owner will not be enough without more – there must be unless there has been a sufficient detriment[34]; and secondly, this point was seemingly developed by Chadwick L.J. in *Oxley v Hiscock* when the latter stipulated at the start of paragraph 68 of his judgment that his decision applies to cases where the 'common features' include the fact that each party "*makes some financial contribution to the purchase*".[35] It is submitted that, in *Oxley v Hiscock*, Chadwick LJ was clarifying (amongst other things) was that *provided* both parties made financial contributions to the purchase the absence of a discussion is not fatal. Assuming such a financial contribution was made, that satisfied the test for detrimental reliance. There does not always have to be an express conversation.

37. Next, assuming that the Court's answer to the first question is "yes, there was a common intention" – either because there was a financial contribution to the purchase, or better still an actual discussion as well – we then come to the second question. The second question is: "what is the extent of the parties' respective beneficial interests in the property? "[36] Here, Chadwick L.J. held that, in many cases, the answer to this question will be supplied by the discussions which the parties had. But, where there is no evidence of any discussion between them as to the amount of the share which each was to have (or even where both parties

34 Ibid, [1991] 1 AC 107 at P131-132, where, in the context of Mrs Rossett having done a very limited amount of work to the renovation of the property, he said: "*I should myself have had considerable doubt whether Mrs. Rosset's contribution to the work of renovation was sufficient to support a claim to a constructive trust in the absence of writing to satisfy the requirements of section 51 of the Law of Property Act 1925 even if her husband's intention to make a gift to her of half or any other share in the equity of the property had been clearly established or if he had clearly represented to her that that was what he intended.*"

35 See above as quoted; or para 68 of the judgment. However,

36 Ibid, para 69.

candidly accept they did not discuss it at all), the Court must supply the answer. And the answer then becomes "*that each is entitled to that share which the court considers fair having regard to the whole course of dealing between them in relation to the property.*" The whole course of conduct may include arrangements which go beyond initial financial contributions, to include other outgoings or dealings over time.

38. In the result, Chadwick L.J. held that the trial judge had not been required to apply the resulting trust doctrine and hold that the property was held in shares proportionate to their contributions as point of acquisition. Equally, however, the judge had erred in concluding that on the facts of the case that the parties had intended to hold the property in equal shares. Having regard to their relative contributions to the purchase price and to the whole course of their dealing, his Lordship decided that the fair division of the proceeds of sale would be 60% to Mr Hiscock and 40% to Miss Oxley.

Stack v Dowden

39. Together with *Jones v Kernott* [2012] AC 776 (see later in this Chapter), *Stack v Dowden*[37] is undoubtedly now the leading authority on the common intention constructive trust.

40. The House of Lords appeal in *Stack v Dowden* took place in February of 2007, relatively soon after the appeal in the Court of Appeal in *Oxley v Hiscock*[38]. Like *Oxley v Hiscock,* it concerned a domestic cohabitation appeal between an unmarried man and women, who had children together. *Stack v Dowden,* however, was a *joint names* case whereas *Oxley v Hiscock* was a sole name case, albeit one where there was no doubt that Miss

---

37 [2007] 2 AC 432.

38 As to *Oxley v Hiscock*, see earlier in this Chapter.

Oxley had made capital contributions. As Lady Hale acknowledged in her speech, unlike Mr Stack and Miss Dowden's case, Miss Oxley had had "*first to surmount the hurdle of showing that she had any beneficial interest at all, before showing exactly what that interest was.*"[39] In *Stack v Dowden*, the parties were "*not concerned with the first hurdle*[40]", because it was a joint names case.

41. As to the wider question of quantification – traced back to *Lloyds Bank v Rosset* Lady Hale recognised (as did Lord Walker) that:

> "*there is undoubtedly an argument for saying, as did the Law Commission in Sharing Homes, A Discussion Paper, para 4.23 that the observations, which were strictly obiter dicta, of Lord Bridge of Harwich in Lloyds Bank plc v Rosset [1991] 1 AC 107 have set that hurdle rather too high in certain respects. But that does not concern us now. It is common ground that a conveyance into joint names is sufficient, at least in the vast majority of cases, to surmount the first hurdle. The question is whether, that hurdle surmounted, the approach to quantification should be the same.*[41]"

42. The facts of *Stack v Dowden* were as follows. The claimant – and appellant in the House of Lords – was Mr Stack. The defendant – and respondent to the appeal – was Miss Dowden. The parties began a relationship in 1975. In 1983, Miss Dowden bought a house in her sole name in which the parties lived together as if husband and wife and over time they had four children. Miss Dowden, who throughout their time together earned more money than Mr Stack – and sometimes almost twice as much – made all the payments due under the

39 [2007] 2 AC 432, P 455 at para 61.

40 Ibid at 456 para 63.

41 Ibid, para 63.

mortgage and paid the household bills on that property. The parties also did a great deal of work towards improving the property and in 1993 it was sold for about three times the figure that Miss Dowden had originally paid for it. A second property was then purchased as their family home – and this time it was conveyed into their joint names. Over 65% of the purchase price was paid from Miss Dowden's proceeds of sale from the first property, in which they had both lived. She had paid those proceeds of sale into her sole account, but now applied them towards the joint purchase. The balance of the purchase price was made up of a mortgage in the parties' joint names and two endowment policies, one in their joint names and one in Miss Dowden's sole name. Mr Stack paid the mortgage interest and the premiums due under the endowment policy held in their joint names and Miss Dowden paid the premiums due under the endowment policy held in her sole name. Moreover, the parties always kept separate bank accounts and made separate savings and investments. Over the course of their years in the property together the joint mortgage was paid off by a series of lump sum payments of which Miss Dowden provided just under 60% of the capital.

43. The parties separated in 2002 and Mr Stack left the property while the Miss Dowden remained there with the children. Mr Stack successfully applied to the judge for, inter alia, an order for sale of the property and an equal division of the proceeds. The Court of Appeal allowed Miss Dowden's appeal and ordered that the net proceeds of sale be divided 65% to 35% in her favour.

44. The House of Lords dismissed the appeal and affirmed the decision of the Court of Appeal ([2006] 1 FLR 254), albeit on different grounds. The majority of the Appellate Committee of the House were persuaded by the fact that Miss Dowden had contributed far more to the acquisition of the house than had Mr Stack; that the parties had never pooled their separate fin-

ancial resources for the common good and accordingly everything, apart from the house and associated endowment policy, had been kept strictly separate. Because of that, they held, the case was highly unusual insofar as the parties kept their affairs rigidly separate. All of those factors culminated in the strong inference that the parties had not intended their shares in the property to be equal. Accordingly, Miss Dowden had made good her case for a 65% share of the beneficial interest, and Mr Stack's appeal was dismissed.

45. As aforesaid, the undoubted leading speech is that of Lady Hale, with whom the majority agreed (4 - 1). She was supported in particular by Lord Walker. The sole dissenting judgment was that of Lord Neuberger. To better understand this crucial decision, we will consider each of these speeches separately.

Lady Hale's Speech

46. Lady Hale's speech begins at Paragraph 40 of the reported case. She discussed the development of the law, and the social and economic context behind it. She set out how the TR1 Form was introduced, in April 1998, which provides a box for the transferees to declare whether they are to hold the property on trust for themselves as joint tenants, or on trust for themselves as tenants in common in equal shares, or on some other trusts which are inserted on the form. She noted that, if Box 10 on the TR1 form was invariably completed, the problem confronting the parties like Mr Stack and Miss Dowden would eventually disappear[42].

42 Of course, the busy TOLATA practitioner will still have to deal with: (1) the very many cases where properties were acquired before April 1997, although in joint names cases there is now the *Stack* presumption of a joint tenancy; (2) cases since 1997 where the TR1 form was not fully completed before a property purchase; (3) cases where there is an argument concerning a change of intentions; (4) cases concerning the timing of an order for sale and/or cross Schedule 1 applications; and, of course, (5) cases necessitating the giving of sometimes unwelcome but fundamental legal advice to

(1) Equity follows the law

47. At paragraphs [53] and [54] of her speech, Lady Hale poses the question:

> *[53] "... In what circumstances should it be expected that, independently of the information required by the Land Registry forms, joint transferees would execute a declaration of trust? Is it when they intend that the beneficial interests should be the same as the legal interests or when they intend that they should be different?*
>
> *[54] At first blush, the answer appears obvious. It should only be expected that joint transferees would have spelt out their beneficial interests when they intended them to be different from their legal interests. Otherwise, it should be assumed that equity follows the law and that the beneficial interests reflect the legal interests in the property. I do not think that this proposition is controversial, even in old fashioned unregistered conveyancing. It has even more force in registered conveyancing in the consumer context...."*
>
> ....
>
> *[56] Just as the starting point where there is sole legal ownership is sole beneficial ownership, the starting point where there is joint legal ownership is joint beneficial ownership. The onus is upon the person seeking to show that the beneficial ownership is different from the legal ownership. So in sole ownership cases it is upon the non-owner to show that he has any interest at all. In joint ownership cases, it is upon the joint owner who claims to have other than a joint beneficial interest*."*

aggrieved parties who made unequal contributions to a joint purchase when times were good but who become upset about having done so when the relationship turns sour.

> …
>
> *[58] For the reasons already stated, at least in the domestic consumer context, a conveyance into joint names indicates both legal and beneficial joint tenancy, unless and until the contrary is proved*.*
>
> (*author's emphasis)

48. Accordingly, the presumption that equity follows the law was made clear.

(2) Context is everything

49. But if the starting point is that equity follows the law, how is the contrary to be proved? Should it be by way of the resulting trust, or the constructive trust? At paragraph 59, Lady Hale begins the next part of her judgment, analysing and ruling out the presumption of the resulting trust.

> *[59] The question is, how, if at all, is the contrary to be proved? Is the starting point the presumption of resulting trust, under which shares are held in proportion to the parties' financial contributions to the acquisition of the property, unless the contributor or contributors can be shown to have had a contrary intention? Or is it that the contrary can be proved by looking at all the relevant circumstances in order to discern the parties' common intention?*
>
> *[60] The presumption of resulting trust is not a rule of law. According to Lord Diplock in Pettitt v Pettitt [1970] AC 777, 823h, the equitable presumptions of intention are "no more than a consensus of judicial opinion disclosed by reported cases as to the most likely inference of fact to be drawn in the absence of any evidence to the contrary"....*

50. Her Ladyship approved of the decision in *Oxley v Hiscock*. She referred to and quoted from the judgment of Chadwick L.J. (cited earlier in this Chapter), where his Lordship set out the principles of fairness at the quantification stage if the parties' intentions were unclear. Lady Hale put it this way:

> "*The law has indeed moved on in response to changing social and economic conditions. The search is to ascertain the parties' shared intentions, actual, inferred or imputed, with respect to the property in the light of their whole course of conduct in relation to it.*[43]"

51. Lady Hale was building towards a conclusion favouring the constructive trust approach. But what of difference between joint names and sole name cases? Does that make a difference? She said:

> *[65] "... The approach to quantification in cases where the home is conveyed into joint names should certainly be no stricter than the approach to quantification in cases where it has been conveyed into the name of one only....*

52. However, she warned:

> *[66] "...the questions in a joint names case are not simply "what is the extent of the parties' beneficial interests?" but "did the parties intend their beneficial interests to be different from their legal interests?" and "if they did, in what way and to what extent?" There are differences between sole and joint names cases when trying to divine the common intentions or understanding between the parties. I know of no case in which a sole legal owner (there being no declaration of trust) has been held to hold the property on a beneficial joint tenancy. But a court may well hold that joint legal owners*

43 Ibid, P.455 at para 60.

(there being no declaration of trust) are also beneficial joint tenants. Another difference is that it will almost always have been a conscious decision to put the house into joint names. Even if the parties have not executed the transfer, they will usually, if not invariably, have executed the contract which precedes it. Committing oneself to spend large sums of money on a place to live is not normally done by accident or without giving it a moment's thought.

[67] "…Mortgagees used to insist upon the home being put in the name of the person whom they assumed would be the main breadwinner. Nowadays, they tend to think that it is in their best interests that the home be jointly owned and both parties assume joint and several liability for the mortgage. (It is, of course, a matter of indifference to the mortgagees where the beneficial interests lie.) Here again, this factor does not invalidate the parties' choice if there is an express declaration of trust, nor should it automatically count against it where there is none.

[68] "The burden will therefore be on the person seeking to show that the parties did intend their beneficial interests to be different from their legal interests, and in what way. This is not a task to be lightly embarked upon. In family disputes, strong feelings are aroused when couples split up. These often lead the parties, honestly but mistakenly, to reinterpret the past in self-exculpatory or vengeful terms. They also lead people to spend far more on the legal battle than is warranted by the sums actually at stake. A full examination of the facts is likely to involve disproportionate costs. In joint names cases it is also unlikely to lead to a different result unless the facts are very unusual…"

53. Lady Hale drove towards her conclusion:

[69] "In law, "context is everything" and the domestic context is very different from the commercial world. Each case will

turn on its own facts. Many more factors than financial contributions may be relevant to divining the parties' true intentions. These include: any advice or discussions at the time of the transfer which cast light upon their intentions then; the reasons why the home was acquired in their joint names; the reasons why (if it be the case) the survivor was authorised to give a receipt for the capital moneys; the purpose for which the home was acquired; the nature of the parties' relationship; whether they had children for whom they both had responsibility to provide a home; how the purchase was financed, both initially and subsequently; how the parties arranged their finances, whether separately or together or a bit of both; how they discharged the outgoings on the property and their other household expenses. When a couple are joint owners of the home and jointly liable for the mortgage, the inferences to be drawn from who pays for what may be very different from the inferences to be drawn when only one is owner of the home. The arithmetical calculation of how much was paid by each is also likely to be less important. It will be easier to draw the inference that they intended that each should contribute as much to the household as they reasonably could and that they would share the eventual benefit or burden equally. The parties' individual characters and personalities may also be a factor in deciding where their true intentions lay. In the cohabitation context, mercenary considerations may be more to the fore than they would be in marriage, but it should not be assumed that they always take pride of place over natural love and affection. At the end of the day, having taken all this into account, cases in which the joint legal owners are to be taken to have intended that their beneficial interests should be different from their legal interests will be very unusual.

[70] This is not, of course, an exhaustive list. There may also be reason to conclude that, whatever the parties' intentions at the outset, these have now changed. An example might be where one party has financed (or constructed himself) an

extension or substantial improvement to the property, so that what they have now is significantly different from what they had then.

54. Lady Hale's speech – and in particular the seminal part quoted above that "*context is everything*" – means that following S*tack v Dowden* more factors than mere financial contributions to the acquisition of title of the property are likely to be important. It was therefore with this metaphorical swing of the axe that the presumption of the resulting trust was, if not completely killed off, at least incapacitated in most circumstances. It is certainly dead to all extents and purposes in the domestic cohabitation context[44].

55. The busy practitioner may also wish to note that the factors discussed in Lady Hale's speech at paragraph 69 actually form a very helpful practical checklist of the factors that should be explored with clients in conference.

56. It is somewhat easier if one looks at the factors in bullet point format. Those giving advice and taking instructions may wish to consider some or all of the following with a new client:

- *What, if any, advice did the parties receive at the time of the transfer which might cast light upon their intentions at that stage?*
- *What, if any, discussions did the parties have with each other at the time of the transfer which might cast light upon their intentions at that stage?*
- *Why the home was acquired in their joint names?*

44 Unless, in a rare case, the parties may be both joint domestic and business partners, per *Stack v Dowden* at para 32 and *Jones v Kernott* at para 31.

- *Why (if applicable) does the transfer state that the survivor is authorised to give a receipt for the capital moneys*[45]*?*
- *For what purpose was the home acquired?*
- *What was the nature of the parties' relationship?*
- *Do or did the parties have children for whom they both had responsibility to provide a home?*
- *How was the purchase price financed, both initially and subsequently?*
- *How did the parties arrange their finances; was it separately or together or a bit of both?*
- *How did the parties discharge the outgoings on the property and their other household expenses?*
- *Were both parties paying as much as they could reasonably be expected towards the mortgage and/or other household outgoings?*
- *What were the parties' individual characters and personalities like?*

57. Applying the law to the facts of Stack v Dowden, Lady Hale said that "*this is not a case in which it can be said that the parties pooled their separate resources, even notionally, for the common good.*[46]" The parties even undertook separate responsibility for

45 Although it should be said for completeness that Lady Hale was clear that unless the parties could be shown by evidence to have fully understood the significance of this, it should not lead by itself to an inference that the parties had intended a joint tenancy, per paragraphs 51 and 84; and see also *Huntingford v Hobbs* [1993] 1 FLR 736.

46 Ibid, P464, para 90.

distinct parts of their expenditure relating to their children. It was impossible to deduce a commitment that each would pay what they could.

58. And so to the result. The general presumption is that equity follows the law, or in other words that the beneficial interests follow the legal interests unless and until the contrary can be proven (which, in most cases, is to be very difficult). So *Stack v Dowden* ironically created that rule, but then the unusual facts of that case were a cause to make an immediate exception to it.

Lord Walker's speech

59. As has been pointed out elsewhere in this work[47], Lord Walker's speech agrees with Lady Hale, and provided something of a supplementary judgment crossed with an historical commentary. Lord Walker's speech is well worth adding to the practitioner's extended reading list - it provides a detailed yet accessible tour through the case history. For present purposes, the following short segments shall suffice. First of all, at paragraph 26, Lord Walker opined that:

> *"...Lord Bridge's extreme doubt [in Rosset] "whether anything less will do" was certainly consistent with many first-instance and Court of Appeal decisions.... [and] ... whether or not Lord Bridge's observation was justified in 1990, in my opinion the law has moved on, and your Lordships should move it a little more in the same direction, while bearing in mind that the Law Commission may soon come forward with proposals which, if enacted by Parliament, may recast the law in this area."*

60. Lord Walker firmly supported Lady Hale on the question of the burden of proof. He added:

47 See the beginning of this Chapter.

> *[33] In the ordinary domestic case where there are joint legal owners there will be a heavy burden in establishing to the court's satisfaction that an intention to keep a sort of balance-sheet of contributions actually existed, or should be inferred, or imputed to the parties. The presumption will be that equity follows the law. In such cases the court should not readily embark on the sort of detailed examination of the parties' relationship and finances that was attempted (with limited success) in this case. I agree with Lady Hale that this is, on its facts, an exceptional case.*

61. Lord Walker did not, however, go into a detailed exposition of the difference between an inference and imputation in Stack v Dowden. Neither did Lady Hale. That was later dealt with in *Jones v Kernott*, as to which see below.

62. As to the question of contributions "*referable to the acquisition of the house*" – a concept espoused by Lord Diplock in *Gissing v Gissing, Lord Walker questioned the use of the word "referable". He said:*

> *[34] "... 'Referable' is a word of wide and uncertain meaning. It would not assist the development of the law to go back to the sort of difficulties that arose in connection with the doctrine of part performance, where the act of part performance relied on had to be "uniquely referable" to a contract of the sort alleged.... Now that almost all houses and flats are bought with mortgage finance, and the average period of ownership of a residence is a great deal shorter than the contractual term of the mortgage secured on it, the process of buying a house does very often continue, in a real sense, throughout the period of its ownership. The law should recognise that by taking a wide view of what is capable of counting as a contribution towards the acquisition of a residence, while remaining sceptical of the value of alleged improvements that are really insignificant, or elaborate argu-*

ments (suggestive of creative accounting) as to how the family finances were arranged.

[35] That is in my view the way in which the law can be seen developing through a considerable number of decisions of the Court of Appeal, of which I would single out Grant v Edwards [1986] Ch 638 (before Lloyds Bank plc v Rosset [1991] 1 AC 107) and then Stokes v Anderson [1991] 1 FLR 391, Midland Bank plc v Cooke [1995] 2 All ER 562 and Oxley v Hiscock [2005] Fam 211. In the last-mentioned case Chadwick LJ summarised the law as follows, at para 69, Lord Bridge's "second category" cases):

"But, in a case where there is no evidence of any discussion between them as to the amount of the share which each was to have-and even in a case where the evidence is that there was no discussion on that point-the question still requires an answer. It must now be accepted that (at least in this court and below) the answer is that each is entitled to that share which the court considers fair having regard to the whole course of dealing between them in relation to the property. And, in that context, 'the whole course of dealing between them in relation to the property' includes the arrangements which they make from time to time in order to meet the outgoings (for example, mortgage contributions, council tax and utilities, repairs, insurance and housekeeping) which have to be met if they are to live in the property as their home."

63. The reader will note that Chadwick L.J.'s judgment in *Oxley v Hiscock* is being repeated once again. As aforesaid, its importance to the development of this area of the law cannot be underestimated.

64. There were also helpful words of clarification by Lord Walker about the extent to which contributions by way of improvements to a property might be relevant:

"...I would only add that Chadwick LJ did not refer to contributions in kind in the form of manual labour on improvements, possibly because that was not an issue in that case. For reasons already mentioned, I would include contributions in kind by way of manual labour, provided that they are significant.[48]

Lord Neuberger's dissenting speech

65. The dissenting judgement of Lord Neuberger flew the flag for the last stand of the resulting trust, at least in the domestic context. His Lordship expressed the view that it was:

"... inappropriate for the law when applied to cases of this sort to depart from the well-established principles laid down over the years. It also seems to me that the law of resulting and constructive trusts is flexible enough to deal with problems such as those thrown up by cases such as this, and it would be a disservice to the important causes of certainty and consistency if we were to hold otherwise. I note that the Court of Appeal's recent decisions in this case and in Oxley v Hiscock [2005] Fam 211 (both of which were rightly decided) produced an outcome which would be dictated by a resulting trust solution.[49]

66. Lord Neuberger was particularly critical of the evolution of the difference between an inference and an imputation. At the very least, he set out clearly the difference between the two concepts:

"An inferred intention is one which is objectively deduced to be the subjective actual intention of the parties, in the light of their actions and statements. An imputed intention is one which is attributed to the parties, even though no such actual intention can be deduced from their actions and statements,

48 Ibid, per Lord Walker, P448 at para 36.

49 Ibid, per Lord Neuberger at P 467, at para 106.

and even though they had no such intention. Imputation involves concluding what the parties would have intended, whereas inference involves concluding what they did intend.[50]"

67. Lord Neuberger said that to impute an intention would:

"*... not only be wrong in principle and a departure from two decisions of your Lordships' House in this very area, but it also would involve a judge in an exercise which was difficult, subjective and uncertain. (Hence the advantage of the resulting trust presumption.) It would be difficult because the judge would be constructing an intention where none existed at the time, and where the parties may well not have been able to agree. It would be subjective for obvious reasons. It would be uncertain because it is unclear whether one considers a hypothetical negotiation between the actual parties, or what reasonable parties would have agreed.*[51]"

68. As to the contextual approach, Lord Neuberger was in opposition to the approach preferred by Lady Hale. His Lordship commented:

"*I am unimpressed, for instance, by the argument that, merely because they have already lived together for a long time sharing all regular outgoings, including those in respect of the previous property they occupied, the parties must intend that the beneficial interest in the home they are acquiring, with differently sized contributions, should be held in equal shares. Particularly where the parties have chosen not to marry, their close and loving relationship does not by any means necessarily imply an intention to share all their assets equally. There is a large difference between sharing outgoings and making a gift of a valuable share in property; outgoings*

50 Ibid, at para 126.

51 Ibid, at para 127.

are relatively small regular sums arising out of day-to-day living, but an interest in the home is a capital asset, with a substantial value. I am similarly unconvinced that the ownership of the beneficial interest in a home acquired in joint names is much affected by whether the parties have children at the time of acquisition. While it justifies the obvious inference that it is to be used for the children as well as the parties, it says nothing on its own as to the intended ownership of the beneficial interest.[52]"

69. One point on which Lord Neuberger did agree with Lord Walker and Lady Hale – although the latter did not have cause on the facts to explore this point in any detail – was that of capital improvements. Lord Neuberger said:

> "*I agree with Lord Walker that … the fact that one party carries out significant improvements to the home will justify an adjustment of the apportionment of the beneficial interest in his favour. In such a case, the cost could be seen as capital expenditure which differs from regular outgoings relating to the use of the home, and is not dissimilar in financial effect, from the cost of acquiring the home in the first place. To qualify, any work must be substantial: decoration or repairs (at least unless they were very significant) would not do.*"[53]

70. One other interesting feature of Lord Neuberger's speech was that he used almost a reverse logic to explain why his approach could be fairer than the constructive trust approach. With regards to the repayment of a mortgage in joint names, Lord Neuberger thought that "*in some cases, repayments of capital could have the effect of adjusting the shares in the beneficial interest. (It is conceivable that that could apply to payments of interest as well).*" But, as he qualified:

52 Ibid at P473-474, para 132.

53 Ibid at P475, para 139

> *"In many cases, the repayments of capital, even if effected wholly by one party, should not be interpreted as indicating an intention to alter the way in which the beneficial interest is apportioned. Thus, the fact that one party is the home-maker (and, often, child-carer) and the other is the wage-earner would probably not justify the former having his share decreased simply because the other party repays the mortgage by instalments, but it may be different where both parties earn and share the home-making, but one of them repays the mortgage by a single capital sum.[54]"*

Post Stack v Dowden

71. Perhaps regrettably, the decision in Stack v Dowden did not resolve all of the complexity of this area of the law. Indeed, some argued at the time that it raised a number of questions. But to start with, let us consider with what we *did* glean from the outcome. First, we learnt that Lord Neuberger's favoured position of the resulting trust was <u>not</u> to be the way forward, at least in domestic cohabitation cases. Secondly, we learnt that <u>equity follows the law</u> and <u>the starting point in a joint names case is an equal beneficial interest</u> absent a deed of trust (or, rarely, some other form of cogent evidence) to the contrary. We learned that many more factors than mere financial contributions may be relevant to divining the parties' intentions.

72. In terms of the unresolved questions, the position in sole name cases was not made wholly clear, at least to the minds of many at the time. Secondly, the legal profession had to quickly get to grips with the apparent difference between inference and imputation, but the extent of the application of each was unclear. When precisely should one use the former and when, if at all, could one use the latter? Thirdly, *Stack v Dowden* held that equity follows the law, but then immediately broke its own

54 Ibid, at P. 476-477, para 140.

rule to hold that Miss Dowden had a 65% share to Mr Stack's 35%, despite them being joint legal owners. So how hard is it really to rebut the presumption of beneficial joint ownership? And fourthly, beyond a fleeting reference to the question of the parties potentially changing their intentions – in Lady Hale's speech – the decision did not provide any great detail of the circumstances in which common intention may change over time.

Jones v Kernott

73. Thus, the appeal in *Jones v Kernott*[55] gave the newly renamed Supreme Court a fresh opportunity to revisit the decision and principles set out in *Stack v Dowden*. As the conclusion to the last part of the chapter revealed, *Stack v Dowden* left some significant general questions outstanding. In the intervening period, there were several cases which were helpful[56], but none had reached the Supreme Court and provided the opportunity to give the guidance which *Jones v Kernott* was to go on to set out.

74. The Supreme Court judgment in *Jones v Kernott* is in some respects remarkable. It takes the form of a joint judgment by Lady Hale and Lord Walker (which was then and still is a relatively rare event). In their joint judgment, Lady Hale and Lord Walker seek to refine and contextualise their speeches in *Stack v Dowden*. There is, in part, a refutation of some of the academic articles criticising that decision. And there is a lengthy recitation

55 [2012] 1 AC 776

56 For example, *Fowler v Baron* [2008] 2 FLR 831 where in a joint names case the Court of Appeal was able to infer, after Stack v Dowden, that despite Miss Fowler not having made a contribution to the purchase price or the mortgage repayments on her home with Mr Baron, there was other evidence (e.g. mutual wills) which supported the inference that they each intended the other to hold the beneficial shares in the property (equally). Separately, and of some assistance in sole name cases, was the Privy Council decision in *Abbott v Abbott* [2008] 1 FLR 1451.

of both the facts and the correct interpretation of the decision in *Stack v Dowden*. Indeed, it is not until almost half way through the judgment that the facts of Miss Jones' and Mr Kernott's case are first mentioned.

75. So what issues were explored? Four primary questions arose from the decision in *Stack v Dowden*. First, did the constructive trust undoubtedly triumph over the resulting trust in domestic cohabitation cases? Secondly, is there a single regime for joint names cases and sole name cases? Thirdly, at what stage (if arguably at all) is the Court entitled to impute to the parties an intention which they 'never had'? And fourthly, in what circumstances may the parties' intentions change?

76. With the benefit of hindsight, some of the above answers to the questions posed may now seem elementary. But at the time there was, sadly, a great deal of confusion amongst lawyers in private practice as to the extent of the decision in *Stack v Dowden*. The decision in *Jones* arguably consolidated Lady Hale's popularity amongst family lawyers not only because she recognised and dealt with these criticisms head on, but also because she took the opportunity to clarify the law not just in relation to joint names cases but also *sole name cases* – notwithstanding the fact that no sole name case had reached the Supreme Court or its predecessor since *Lloyds Bank v Rosset* in 1991.

77. The first question was whether constructive trust triumphed over the resulting trust? While one would think (perhaps with the benefit of hindsight) that the answer to that question was obvious from *Stack v Dowden*, Lady Hale did not actually put it quite that explicitly.[57] Lady Hale and Lord Walker therefore

57 As Lady Hale recognises in paragraph 23 of her joint speech in Kernott v Jones, noting that the only such explicit reference to the same in *Stack v Dowden* was in Lord Walker's concurring judgment in *Stack* at paragraph 31 therein.

took the opportunity in *Jones v Kernott* to make the position abundantly clear, at paragraph 25, when they said:

> *"The time has come to make it clear, in line with* Stack v Dowden *(see also Abbott v Abbott [2007] UKPC 53, [2008] 1 FLR 1451), that in the case of the purchase of a house or flat in joint names for joint occupation by a married or unmarried couple, where both are responsible for any mortgage, there is no presumption of a resulting trust arising from their having contributed to the deposit (or indeed the rest of the purchase) in unequal shares..."*

78. Was this almost an admission by the Supreme Court that it did not 'spell out' clearly enough in *Stack v Dowden* that the constructive trust would definitely now apply (and accordingly the presumption of a resulting trust would not apply) in cohabitation cases? In fairness to the Supreme Court (or the House of Lords, as it still was called in *Stack)* that conclusion was apparent (or should have been, to the keen eye) from the decision in *Stack* precisely because, as Lady Hale clarified in *Jones*, it is "*not possible at one and the same time to have a presumption or starting point of joint beneficial interests and a presumption (let alone a rule) that the parties' beneficial interests are in proportion to their respective financial contributions.*"[58]

79. The second question was whether or not there is a single regime for joint names cases and sole name cases. Lady Hale and Lord Walker dealt with this under a separate sub-heading, at paragraph 16 onwards. They make the introductory point that, as a generality, both sole name cases and joint names cases are governed by the law of trusts[59]. But, more pertinently, they then explicitly stated that:

---

58 Lady Hale in *Jones v Kernott* [2012] 1 AC 776 at 786, para 23.

59 Ibid, at 783, para 16.

> *"To the extent that we recognise that a "common intention" trust is of central importance to "joint names" as well as "single names" cases, we are going some way to meet that hope. Nevertheless it is important to point out that the starting point for analysis is different in the two situations. That is so even though it may be necessary to enquire into the varied circumstances and reasons why a house or flat has been acquired in a single name or in joint names (they range, for instance, from Lowson v Coombes [1999] Ch 373, where the property was in the woman's sole name because the man was apprehensive of claims by his separated wife, to Adekunle v Ritchie [2007] WTLR 1505, where an enfranchised freehold was in joint names because the elderly tenant could not obtain a mortgage on her own)."*

80. However, the starting point in each type of case is necessarily different. It is different because in a sole name case, "*the claimant whose name is not on the proprietorship register has the burden of establishing some sort of implied trust, normally what is now termed a "common intention" constructive trust.*"[60] In other words, the claimant in such a case as to prove that they were intended to have any interest *at all*, unlike, for example, in *Stack v Dowden* where both parties already were joint legal owners and had therefore already surmounted this hurdle by default.

81. At paragraph 52 of their joint speech, Lady Hale and Lord Walker conclude this point in the following way:

> *"This case[61] is not concerned with a family home which is put into the name of one party only. The starting point is different. The first issue is whether it was intended that the other party have any beneficial interest in the property at all.[62] If he does, the second issue is what that interest is. There is no pre-*

60 Ibid at 784, para 17.

61 i.e. *Jones v Kernott.*

sumption of joint beneficial ownership. But their common intention has once again to be deduced objectively from their conduct. If the evidence shows a common intention to share beneficial ownership but does not show what shares were intended, the court will have to proceed as at para 51(4) and (5) above[63]*."*

82. The third question which remained unanswered from *Stack v Dowden* was particularly tricky. It concerned the stage at which the court is entitled to impute to the parties an intention which they 'never had'. Even in *Jones v Kernott*[64], Lord Wilson's speech demonstrates that the distinction between inference and imputation is hard to identify (see paragraphs 85-88). That is demonstrated by the fact that the three Justices in the majority were able to *infer* a common intention that the parties' shares would vary to 90% to 10%, whereas the two dissenting two Justices (Lord Wilson and Lord Kerr) would have reached the same result but on the basis of an *imputation.*

---

62 For a sole name case worthy of further reading, see *Thompson v Hurst* [2014] 1 FLR 238, in which the parties had intended to buy a property together, but after receiving the advice of a mortgage advisor proceeded in the name of the respondent only. The trial judge and the Court of Appeal, who unanimously upheld the decision, found that the fact that the parties had explored purchasing a property together but then did not go on to do so was not necessarily evidence of a firm common intention to hold a property in equal shares. In the absence of a joint purchase, the simple fact of the matters was that there was no scope to presume that the parties had intended a joint tenancy both in law and equity. The decision of the court, after a 20-year relationship with children, saw the claimant only awarded a 10% share on the basis of imputation. At first sight, that might appear capricious, but the Court of Appeal was satisfied that the judge had reached a fair outcome on the facts of that particular case, which she had analysed in an "exemplary fashion".

63 A reference to imputation, as to which see later in this chapter.

64 Of which the ratio decidendi was decided by a 3-2 majority comprising Lady Hale, Lord Walker and Lord Collins.

83. Dealing with this point, Lady Hale and Lord Walker noted that in *Gissing v Gissing*[65], even the House of Lords were "*singularly unresponsive to each other*", adding "*We can only guess at the order in which the speeches were composed.*"[66] Lady Hale and Lord Walker appeared determined to draw a line under the past: "*[Gissing] was 40 years ago and we are now another generation on.*" In looking to the future, Lady Hale and Lord Walker set out the essence of their Speeches in *Stack v Dowden*, and then compared them contextually with Lord Neuberger and Rimer LJ's dissenting speeches in *Stack* and in the Court of Appeal in *Jones v Kernott* respectively. The drawing together of these competing arguments is worth setting out in full. They said:

> *[30] "The decision in Stack v Dowden produced a division of the net proceeds of sale of the house in shares roughly corresponding to the parties' financial contributions over the years. The majority reached that conclusion by inferring a common intention (see Baroness Hale of Richmond's opinion at para [92], following her detailed analysis of the facts starting at para [86]). Only Lord Neuberger reached the same result by applying the classic resulting trust doctrine (which involved, it is to be noted, imputing an intention to the parties*[67]*)."*

> *[31] "In deference to the comments of Lord Neuberger and Rimer LJ, we accept that the search is primarily to ascertain the parties' actual shared intentions, whether expressed or to be inferred from their conduct. However, there are at least two exceptions. The first, which is not this case, is where the classic resulting trust presumption applies. Indeed, this would be rare in a domestic context, but might perhaps arise where*

65 [1971] AC 886

66 *Jones v Kernott*, Ibid, paragraph 28.

67 It is perhaps ironic that this comment was attributed to Lord Neuberger in *Stack* when he himself expressed himself to be very much against imputation as an evidential exercise in the very same case, see para 125.

domestic partners were also business partners: see Stack v Dowden, para [32]. The second, which for reasons which will appear later, is in our view, also not this case but will arise much more frequently, where it is clear that the beneficial interests are to be shared, but it is impossible to divine a common intention as to the proportions in which they are to be shared. In those two situations, the court is driven to impute an intention to the parties which they may never have had."

84. So there it is: An imputation is the method to be used where it already demonstrably clear that there was a common intention between the parties, but it is impossible to divine precisely what it was. In those circumstances, it is open to the Court to impute an intention to the parties (having regard to what is fair) as to in what proportions they hold the property. Imputation does not override inference. If the parties' shares can be inferred from the evidence, that agreement must be respected and followed. Thus, it is not for the Court to seek to substitute its own view of what is fair for what the parties did actually agree, or what the court has already found as an inference that they agreed[68]. If there is actual evidence as to what the parties' common intention was, then that should be the outcome of the case. Inference fills the gap where there are no express discussions but where the evidence points to an objectively clear conclusion about intentions. Imputation may only be used where – having got to the stage where it is clear that the parties intended that each should have an interest – there is a dearth of evidence from which to infer what the quantum of their shares are supposed to be. In those circumstances, the court is driven to impute shares to the parties, having regard to their whole course of dealing in relation to the property.

---

68 per Lady Hale and Lord Walker at paragraph 46 (and see *Capehorn v Harris* [2016] 2 FLR 1026, where, following *Jones v Kernott,* the Court of Appeal made the same point).

85. The fourth question raised briefly in *Stack v Dowden*[69] but left to be fully answered until *Jones v Kernott* was when the parties' beneficial interests may change. Indeed, that was the principal focus of the appeal. The consideration of this question, and the answer provided by the Supreme Court in *Jones* warrants a detailed consideration of the facts of that case and the outcome of the appeal.

86. Mr Kernott and Miss Jones met in 1980 and formed a relationship. They did not marry. They had two children, one born in 1984 and the other born in 1986. In 1985, the parties bought a house in Essex, 39 Badger Hall Avenue, in their joint names for £30,000. The deposit of £6,000 was paid by the Miss Jones using the balance of the proceeds of sale of a previous property in her sole name. The remainder of the purchase price was raised by an interest-only mortgage supported by an endowment policy. Mr Kernott paid £100 per week towards the household expenses whilst they lived at the first property. Miss Jones paid the mortgage and other household bills out of their joint resources. In 1986, the parties jointly took out a loan of £2,000 to build an extension to the property. Mr Kernott was primarily responsible for building the extension, which increased the value of the property by around 50% of the purchase price.

87. In 1993, they separated. Mr Kernott moved out. From that point forward, Miss Jones assumed sole responsibility for the outgoings on the property. Mr Kernott made no further contribution towards the acquisition of the property and made very

69 In Lady Hale's speech at para 70, where her Ladyship said: "*There may also be reason to conclude that, whatever the parties' intentions at the outset, these have now changed. An example might be where one party has financed (or constructed himself) an extension or substantial improvement to the property, so that what they have now is significantly different from what they had then.*" But unlike in *Jones v Kernott* the Court in *Stack v Dowden* did not have the opportunity to go on to consider this point in any further detail.

little contribution to the maintenance and support of the children.

88. In October 1995, the property was put on the market but failed to sell. The parties cashed in a joint life insurance policy and the proceeds were divided between them to enable Mr Kernott to put down a deposit on a home of his own. In May 1996, Mr Kernott bought a (second) property in his sole name. Thereafter he made all mortgage payments and met other expenses required to maintain that property.

89. In October 2007, Mr Kernott began proceedings in the county court claiming a declaration under Section 14 of the TOLATA. At trial, Miss Jones conceded that in 1993 when the couple separated, there was insufficient evidence to displace the presumption that their beneficial interests in the first property followed the legal title, so that they were then joint tenants in law and equity[70]. However, she instead contended that the purchase of the Mr Kernott's second property, along with other events since the separation, was evidence that their intentions with respect to the beneficial interest in the first property had changed. The judge agreed and held that the claimant was entitled to 90% of the value of the first property.

90. Mr Kernott appealed to the Chancery Division of the High Court. He contended that the judge had been wrong to infer or impute an intention that the parties' beneficial interests should change after their separation and to quantify those in the way which he had considered fair. The deputy judge held that a change in intention could readily be inferred or imputed from the parties' conduct and that, in the absence of any indication by words or conduct as to how their shares should be altered, the appropriate criterion was what he considered to be fair and just. Accordingly, the deputy judge upheld the judge's findings

70 The trial took place after the outcome of the House of Lords' decision in *Stack v Dowden*.

that the first property should be divided as to 90% for Miss Jones and 10% for Mr Kernott.

91. Mr Kernott appealed again. This time, the Court of Appeal by a majority allowed his appeal and declared that the parties owned the contentious property as tenants in common in equal shares.

92. Miss Jones appealed to the Supreme Court. She relied on the following factual points. Mr Kernott moved out of the property in October 1993. By 1993, the parties had cohabited for eight years. After separation, Miss Jones continued to live there for a further fourteen and a half years until the case came to trial at first instance. In 1995, 39 Badger Hall Avenue was put on the market in October 1995 for £69,995 but failed to sell. In a sense, the parties and the courts were assisted by having an idea of the market value of the property proximate to the time of separation. Mr Kernott, as aforesaid, had gone on to purchase his own (effectively second) property in 1996. That property cost him £57,000. The trial judge had found that he was able to afford that property because he was not making any contribution towards the former family home and because he was not making any significant contribution towards the support of his children. By the time of the hearing before the first instance judge, the property was valued at £245,000.

93. Lady Hale and Lord Walker said this, at paragraph 46:

> *[46] … "The primary search must always be for what the parties actually intended, to be deduced objectively from their words and their actions. If that can be discovered, then, as Mr Nicholas Strauss QC pointed out in the High Court, it is not open to a court to impose a solution upon them in contradiction to those intentions, merely because the court considers it fair to do so."*

[47] "In a case such as this, where the parties already share the beneficial interest, and the question is what their interests are and whether their interests have changed, the court will try to deduce what their actual intentions were at the relevant time. It cannot impose a solution upon them which is contrary to what the evidence shows that they actually intended. But if it cannot deduce exactly what shares were intended, it may have no alternative but to ask what their intentions as reasonable and just people would have been, had they thought about it at the time. This is a fallback position which some courts may not welcome, but the court has a duty to come to a conclusion on the dispute put before it."

[48] "In this case, there is no need to impute an intention that the parties' beneficial interests would change, because the judge made a finding that the intentions of the parties did in fact change. At the outset, their intention was to provide a home for themselves and their progeny. But thereafter their intentions did change significantly. He did not go into detail, but the inferences are not difficult to draw. They separated in October 1993. No doubt in many such cases, there is a period of uncertainty about where the parties will live and what they will do about the home which they used to share. This home was put on the market in late 1995 but failed to sell. Around that time a new plan was formed. The life insurance policy was cashed in and Mr Kernott was able to buy a new home for himself. He would not have been able to do this had he still had to contribute towards the mortgage, endowment policy and other outgoings on 39 Badger Hall Avenue. The logical inference is that they intended that his interest in Badger Hall Avenue should crystallise then. Just as he would have the sole benefit of any capital gain in his own home, Ms Jones would have the sole benefit of any capital gain in Badger Hall Avenue. Insofar as the judge did not in so many words infer that this was their intention, it is clearly the intention which reasonable people would have had, had they thought about it at the time. But in our view it is an

intention which he both could and should have inferred from their conduct.

94. Accordingly, Lady Hale and Lord Walker (and Lord Collins, who concurred) all decided that the parties' change of intentions was to have been inferred from their conduct, not imputed.[71] And the outcome? Lady Hale and Lord Walker found that, on their own calculations, their outcome was "*so close to that which the [trial] judge produced that it would be wrong for an appellate court to interfere.*" They decided that:

> *[49] "... If we take the value of the property as £60,000 in late 1993 (or £70,000 in late 1995) and the value in 2008 as £245,000, and share the £60,000 (or £70,000) equally between the parties, but leave the balance to Ms Jones, that gives him £30,000 (£35,000) and her £215,000 (£210,000), roughly 12% (14%) and 88% (86%) respectively. This calculation ignores the mortgage, which may be the correct approach, as in 2008 the mortgage debt was almost fully covered by the endowment policy which was always meant to discharge it. Introducing the mortgage liability in 1993 (or 1995) into the calculation would be to Mr Kernott's disadvantage, because at that stage the endowment policy would not have been sufficient to discharge the debt, so the equity would have been less."*

The ratio decidendi

95. The ratio decidendi in Jones v Kernott was fairly broad in scope.[72] Helpfully, therefore, at paragraphs 51 and 52 of their joint judgment, Lady Hale and Lord Walker summarise the key

71 Lord Kerr and Lord Wilson reached the same opinion as to the disposal of the appeal, but they both thought that the result should be imputed.

72 Indeed, the headnote to the ICLR Appeal Cases report of the case suggests that it may be found in the following particular paragraphs: 25, 31, 33, 36, 46, 47, 51, 55, 64, 68, 78, 86.

principles set out in their judgment. It is essential to read it in full to properly understand the position.

> *[51] … In a case such as this, where a family home is bought in the joint names of a cohabiting couple who are both responsible for any mortgage, but without any express declaration of their beneficial interests:*
>
> *(1) the starting point is that equity follows the law and they are joint tenants both in law and in equity;*
>
> *(2) that presumption can be displaced by showing:*
>
> *(a) that the parties had a different common intention at the time when they acquired the home, or*
>
> *(b) that they later formed the common intention that their respective shares would change;*
>
> *(3) their common intention is to be deduced objectively from their conduct:*
>
> *'the relevant intention of each party is the intention which was reasonably understood by the other party to be manifested by that party's words and conduct notwithstanding that he did not consciously formulate that intention in his own mind or even acted with some different intention which he did not communicate to the other party'*
>
> *(Lord Diplock in Gissing v Gissing 886, 906, 256 and 271 and 269 and 284 respectively). Examples of the sort of evidence which might be relevant to drawing such inferences are given in Stack v Dowden, at para [69];*
>
> *(4) in those cases where it is clear either:*
>
> *(a) that the parties did not intend joint tenancy at the outset,*

or

(b) had changed their original intention, but it is not possible to ascertain by direct evidence or by inference what their actual intention was as to the shares in which they would own the property:

'the answer is that each is entitled to that share which the court considers fair having regard to the whole course of dealing between them in relation to the property':

Chadwick LJ in Oxley v Hiscock [2005] Fam 211, para [69]. In our judgment: 'the whole course of dealing... in relation to the property' should be given a broad meaning, enabling a similar range of factors to be taken into account as may be relevant to ascertaining the parties' actual intentions;

(5) each case will turn on its own facts. Financial contributions are relevant but there are many other factors which may enable the court to decide what shares were either intended (as in case (3)) or fair (as in case (4)).

[52] This case is not concerned with a family home which is put into the name of one party only. The starting point is different. The first issue is whether it was intended that the other party have any beneficial interest in the property at all. If he does, the second issue is what that interest is. There is no presumption of joint beneficial ownership. But their common intention has once again to be deduced objectively from their conduct. If the evidence shows a common intention to share beneficial ownership but does not show what shares were intended, the court will have to proceed as at para [51](4) and [51](5) above.

96. In summary, therefore, *Jones v Kernott* was a significant decision which greatly increased our understanding of the approach advanced in *Stack v Dowden*. Not only do we now understand

that the common intention of the parties may change, but we also had it clarified for us that (1) there is a single common intention constructive trust regime for sole and joint name cases, subject to the obviously different starting point in relation to legal title and where the ensuing burden of proof lies; and (2) the existence of a common intention (if not express) is to be deduced objectively by way of inference. If a common intention is found, but it cannot be inferred in what proportions the parties intended to hold the property, the court must supply the answer by imputation, and this involves the court applying – at least at this stage of the exercise – Chadwick LJ's analysis in *Oxley v Hiscock* that "*each is entitled to that share which the court considers fair having regard to the whole course of dealing between them in relation to the property*".

Common intention – further exploration

97. But let us develop the point about "common intention" a little bit more. What is common intention? How may we determine it? In its purest form, common intention may be obvious to the parties and their legal advisors, perhaps because it was written down in emails or text messages passing between the parties at the time of or in contemplation of their joint but unequally held property purchase (albeit not drawn up in a deed of trust, or there is likely to be little point in litigating against it[73]).

98. However, there is an obvious disconnect between the plain English meaning of 'common intention' and the legal concept that it provides for. No more obvious example could be given than two former cohabitees who each offer their respective legal advisors different versions of the facts of the case, and who both say they "agreed" to something which – now that they have separated – are quite different things, and frequently mutually exclusive. In plain English at least, they cannot have arrived at a plan which was commonly intended. But that is to miss the

73 See *Goodman v Gallant*, Chapter 1.

whole point of the objective inference exercise, stretching back to Lord Diplock in *Gissing v Gissing* and as set out in the ratio decidendi (summarised above) in *Jones v Kernott*. In actual fact, the common intention is to be found in *"the intention which was reasonably understood by the other party to be manifested by that party's words and conduct notwithstanding that he did not consciously formulate that intention in his own mind or even acted with some different intention which he did not communicate to the other party"*[74]

99. Let us consider some practical examples of discerning the parties' so-called common intention. The first and most obvious example is the one given above where, upon a joint purchase of a property *without* a declaration of trust in the TR1 form, there is at least *some other* written evidence which sets out the parties' common intention, as it was encapsulated at or about the time of purchase: for example an exchange of letters, emails, or text messages, or even a scrap of note paper[75]. The second example may be a conversation, with nothing in writing. Picture the scene where two prospective cohabitees, in the heady days approaching the purchase of their first property together, sit down to dinner and, over the meal, discuss verbally the shares in which they were intending to purchase the property. There may be some cases which can be easily resolved without recourse to litigation where each party accurately remembers (and faithfully reports to their respective lawyers) what the outcome of that conversation was. Far harder for the parties, and indeed their lawyers, if each party went away from that dinner table conversation with different interpretations or recollections of what was said.[76] Either way, the object of the exercise for the legal professionals and the courts is to infer what the parties' so-called

74 Jones v Kernot, Ibid, at para 51(3).

75 Indeed, in one particular case, the author can distinctly recall seeing the weekly communal shopping list written elsewhere on the same sheet of paper on which the parties had scribbled down the shares they were each intended to have.

common intention was by reference to their conduct, which as *Stack v Dowden* has clarified may now be made up by more than mere financial contributions alone. TOLATA cases are hard because so much may turn on the oral evidence of the parties, particularly where little if anything was reduced into writing. One frequently needs to succeed on the 'fact' and the 'law' in order to achieve a good result.

100. It is only where it is clear that the parties did not intend to purchase the property as joint beneficial owners – so, a rare care, given what Lady Hale said in *Stack v Dowden* – and the parties respective and unequal shares cannot be readily *inferred* from their conversations and/or conduct that the court may seek to *impute* to the parties an intention which they never had.

101. The hard part is to truly understand and apply properly – and at the appropriate stage of the exercise – the questions of inference[77] and imputation. The worried practitioner can take comfort from the fact that even the Supreme Court was split over this issue and in the end that case was decided by a 3-2 majority of those who preferred to infer the parties' intentions over those who sought to impute them. If the author can

76 The remarks of Lady Hale in *Stack v Dowden* at para 68 are particular apt here: *"In family disputes, strong feelings are aroused when couples split up. These often lead the parties, honestly but mistakenly, to reinterpret the past in self-exculpatory or vengeful terms. They also lead people to spend far more on the legal battle than is warranted by the sums actually at stake. A full examination of the facts is likely to involve disproportionate costs."*

77 In Jones v Kernott, the Supreme Court recognised the difficulty in this exercise. For example, at paragraph 29, where Lady Hale and Lord Walker said: "...*This sort of constructive intention (or any other constructive state of mind), and the difficulties that they raise, are familiar in many branches of the law. Whenever a judge concludes that an individual "intended, or must be taken to have intended," or "knew, or must be taken to have known," there is an elision between what the judge can find as a fact (usually by inference) on consideration of the admissible evidence, and what the law may supply (to fill the evidential gap) by way of a presumption.*"

suggest a mnemonic for reminding oneself of the difference, it would be to take the example of the theoretical 'dinner table' conversation given above. Inference is the exercise of concluding what the parties *did* intend following their discussions over that dinner.[78] Imputation is as if to imagine that the parties *never sat down* to their dinner and the conversation *never* took place. Instead, imputation is the court's way of determining, if the parties *had* sat down to dinner, what they would have thought.

78 Which, to develop this example, need not consist just of the actual words spoken, but by their contemporaneous and subsequent conduct, actions, and financial contributions.

CHAPTER FOUR
EXTENDED CASE LAW

1. Even with the benefit of the decisions in *Stack v Dowden* and *Jones v Kernott*, there are many remaining TOLATA questions to which the answers are uncertain, or at least arguable either way.

2. This Chapter will seek to summarise some of the key cases in which the aforementioned leading decisions have been considered and applied.

3. First of all, some food for thought. We know from *Jones v Kernott* that the parties' intentions, in some cases, may change.[1] We also know that where the parties' intentions change, one first looks to ascertain that change of intentions by an objective deduction – in other words, an inference. Only where it is not possible to ascertain by direct evidence or by inference what their actual intention was as to the change in the parties' shares is the answer to be that each is entitled to that share which the court considers fair having regard to the whole course of dealing between them in relation to the property.[2]

4. We also know the conceptual difference between an inference and an imputation.[3] It is much harder, when analysing a case, to be categoric about the circumstances where the exercise of inference ends for lack of evidence and the process of imputation begins. In *Jones v Kernott*, the trial judge imputed to

---

1 See Chapter 3.

2 Jones v Kernott, Ibid, para 51 (see Chapter 3).

3 Per Lord Neuberger in *Stack v Dowden*, para 126, set out in full in Chapter 3. See also the hypothetical 'dinner table' example given at the conclusion of Chapter 3.

the parties an intention that their shares had varied from an equal share to shares of 90% and 10% respectively. Although his proposed disposal of the case was proven to be more or less right, it was for the wrong reason, for Lady Hale and her colleagues in the majority thought that that same outcome should have been inferred, not imputed, as the outcome was one that the trial judge "*could and should have inferred from their conduct*" [4]. Lady Hale's rationale[5] was that Mr Jones should be entitled to half of the value of the property at or about the time of his departure, but none of the capital growth subsequently, an analysis which more or less matched the trial judge's outcome on quantum but following a different methodology.

5. So how does the practitioner reassure herself that there are no more inferences to be drawn and that they should start the imputation process? How can one say, with any certainty, that someone akin to Mr Kernott walking away from his property 'intended' to give up his claim to capital growth in his share of that property; as opposed to not giving it any thought whatsoever, and so one could look impute an intention. Much will depend on the evidence – of course, all cases do – and it is therefore suggested that detailed instructions must be taken from parties as to what they thought they were doing at the time of and following separation. It is hard, indeed usually impossible[6], to know what was in the other party's mind. The point of ascertaining the so-called common intention, however, is to find the intention which was reasonably understood by the other party to be manifested by that party's words and conduct notwithstanding that he or she did not consciously formulate

4 Jones v Kernott, Ibid, at para 48.

5 *Jones v Kernott*, Ibid, at para 49.

6 Unless of course they expressed it in writing – 'the bitter farewell note'; the terse email; the application for a Family Law Act 1996 order. In the absence of the above, well drafted pre-action correspondence may in some circumstances be able to tease this out the other party's view about common intention before litigation ensues.

that intention in their own mind. Thus it is not necessarily essential to know what a person subjectively thought – their outward actions can still bind them. But this is a developing area of law – and the boundaries are still somewhat fluid. Some errors at first instance will probably continue to be made until the law has become more familiar to parties, their advisors and their tribunals.[7]

6. There are further unanswered questions. Is there a point in time at which arguments over equitable accounting[8] will end and a change of intentions argument may begin? Are they mutually exclusive? Does silence as to intent count against the departed party on either count?

7. Does ceasing to pay towards the previously occupied property amount to a tacit abandonment of one's interests? If so, does that not sit uncomfortably with the general rule that the departed party will not be entitled to an occupation rent so long as the remaining party pays both parties' monthly mortgage repayments on the jointly owned property? At the risk of posing a facetious question, should the departed property have to write an annual letter, reminding the remaining party that they have not foregone their interest in the property, that they stand ready and willing to meet their share of any outgoings, such as repair costs, and that they definitely do not intend to give up their share?

---

7 In the event that a copy of this work ever makes its way into the hands of a deciding tribunal, whether that be on the Bench at first instance or in a private arbitration forum, the author would respectfully suggest that careful findings of fact be made, following which the tribunal should consider whether obvious or otherwise at least reasonable objective conclusions can be drawn from those facts (an inference); and only where they cannot, should the imputation process be embarked upon ('this is what I think they would have thought' / this is what I think would be fair to the parties).

8 See Chapter 5.

8. Insofar as a change of intentions argument is concerned, does it assist the remaining party if the departing party purchases their own new property in their sole name and is seen to 'wash their hands' of the jointly owned property? Yes, if the facts of *Jones v Kernott* are anything to go by. On the other hand, there was no purchase of a 'new' property in *Barnes v Philips*[9] but that did not stop the court in that case varying the parties' shares in their jointly owned property[10]. There is also yet to be a reported instance of a case where a party has sought to perversely argue a change of intentions to try to take advantage of a negative equity to the detriment of a former, remaining cohabitee.

9. Finally, is it open to a court to find that there has been a change of intentions where the parties had in the first instance expressly set out their shares in a deed of trust under a beneficial joint tenancy? To do so would appear to go behind the rule in *Goodman v Gallant*[11] that such a declaration is determinative unless set aside for a vitiating factor. It should be noted that in both *Jones v Kernott*, and *Barnes v Philips*, the properties were both jointly owned but in neither case was there reported to be a formal declaration of trust (both of the relevant properties in those cases were purchased before the advent of the TR1 form). Miss Jones accepted at trial in her case that there must have been a beneficial joint tenancy (given that her trial took place in the immediate aftermath of *Stack v Dowden* – how could she not); and in *Barnes v Philips* the Court of Appeal noted that the parties had bought that property as joint tenants without giving any further detail.

10. But one could fairly easily imagine a situation where parties buy a property together, expressing their beneficial shares in a deed

9 [2016] 2 FLR 1292.

10 For completeness, one may wish to note that Mr Barnes was reported to have other buy-to-let property interests.

11 [1986] Fam. 106 (Court of Appeal). See Chapter 1.

or otherwise in the TR1 Form, only to separate very shortly afterwards and for several years then go by. How can it be fair for parties to be held to a deed which may be, say, fifteen years old, when their relationship of cohabitation lasted, say, one year only?[12] In those circumstances, is it still then open to a court to find that parties' shares may have changed? A new test case is likely to be required to deal with this eventuality, but at the moment *Goodman v Gallant* remains good law.

11. The point is that TOLATA is a developing area of the law, and we may well be a few reported decisions away from certainty in all aspects of its intricacies. However, there have been a number of helpful recent decisions apart following *Stack v Dowden* or *Jones v Kernott* which have served to supplement our understanding of those decisions, or cast further light on niche areas of this subject.

The domestic context

12. There have, unsurprisingly, been a number of reported decisions since *Stack v Dowden* concerning the domestic context. Pity the poor trial judge in *Baron v Fowler*[13] who decided that case on the basis of the resulting trust approach, just six days[14] before the decision of the House of Lords in *Stack v Dowden* was handed down confirming that the constructive trust should be preferred[15]; and in circumstances where Miss Fowler had made

12 Obviously there may be nuances such as the presence of children of the implied purpose of the trust to provide a family home (including for children), but in broad terms, the question the author frames is whether the rule in *Jones v Kernott* can be used to attack an old trust deed on the basis of an alleged change of intentions but where on the face of it the trust deed remains unimpeachable.

13 [2008] 2 FLR 831

14 In a decision dated 19 April 2007.

15 On 25 April 2007.

no capital contribution to the purchase of a property purchased in the parties' joint legal names. The trial judge awarded her no share in the property. Off ran Miss Fowler's lawyers to the Court of Appeal, now safely armed with Lady Hale's new maxims that equity follows the law and that context is everything. In the eventual outcome the Court of Appeal awarded her a 50% share in the property because other contextual factors (e.g. the parties' wills leaving their respective shares to each) demonstrated that their common intention was that Miss Fowler must have been intended at the outset to have a share.

Capehorn v Harris

13. In *Capehorn v Harris*[16], the Court of Appeal had cause to deal with a decision which demonstrates that the law is not always easy to apply correctly. In that case, the parties had cohabited since 1983. Mr Harris ran a business in which Mrs Capehorn worked but was later declared bankrupt. To assist him with his financial difficulties, Mrs Capehorn took over the running of the business and employed *him* to work for *her*, although he continued to be the driving force of the business. Later still, Mrs Capehorn went on to buy two properties, a farm, in 1993, and a house, in 2002. They were both purchased in her sole name. However, she used funds from – what was, by now – *her* business to pay for the deposit on the Farm in 1993. She paid the balance by way of a mortgage in her sole name. She then took out a further mortgage, secured against the farm, to fund the subsequent acquisition of the house. In 2004, Mr Harris, his bankruptcy well behind him, set up a new company in which he held all the shares. On Mrs Capehorn's evidence, in 2007 there was a discussion between the parties about their financial relationship. Mrs Capehorn asserted that it was agreed that she would transfer her business (Mr Harris's old business) to Mr Harris for effective incorporation into Mr Harris's new

16 [2016] 2 FLR 1026

company in exchange for payments by Mr Harris to Mrs Capehorn of £750 per week. Mrs Capehorn's version of events was accepted as truthful by the trial judge. Mrs Capehorn said that there had been no discussion that Mr Harris was due any share in either of the two properties which she had bought in her sole name. The judge accepted this also and found it as a fact. The difficulty was that the trial judge – wrongly, as the Court of Appeal subsequently found – went on to impute an intention that Mr Harris should have a share of the farm. The Judge awarded him a 25% share. Both parties appealed. The Court of Appeal held that the trial judge had approached the situation incorrectly. Having found that there *was an express discussion* between the parties about their finances which specifically included Mrs Capehorn asserting that she did not agree to Mr Harris having a share of her properties; it was not then open to the trial judge to impute an intention which she thought was fair, or, to put it another way, substitute her own view for that which she had found the parties to have held.

14. Sales L.J[17]., sitting in the Court of Appeal, held that[18]:

> *[16]. "In relation to assets acquired by unmarried co-habitees or partners, where an asset is owned in law by one person but another claims to share a beneficial interest in it* *a two stage analysis* *is called for to determine whether a common intention constructive trust arises.*
>
> *First, the person claiming the beneficial interest must show that there was an agreement that he should have a beneficial interest in the property owned by his partner even if there was no agreement as to the precise extent of that interest.*

17 As he then was; Lord Sales JSC took appointment in the Supreme Court on 14 January 2019.

18 Ibid, paragraphs 16 to 18.

Secondly, if such an agreement can be shown to have been made, then absent agreement on the extent of the interest, the court may impute an intention that the person was to have a fair beneficial share in the asset and may assess the quantum of the fair share in the light of all the circumstances: see Oxley v Hiscock, Stack v Dowden, Jones v Kernott.

[17]. There is an important difference between the approach applicable at each stage. At the first stage, an actual agreement has to be found to have been made, which may be inferred from conduct in an appropriate case. At the second stage, the court is entitled to impute an intention that each person is entitled to the share which the court considers fair having regard to the whole course of dealing between them in relation to the property. <u>A court is not entitled to impute an intention to the parties at the first stage in the analysis</u>.

[18]. Unfortunately in this case in the critical part of her judgment, at paragraphs 152 and 153, the judge erroneously elided these two stages...."

15. Accordingly, the Court of Appeal found that the judge below was wrong to 'look at the matter in the round' and to impute an intention to that Mr Harris was to have had a 25% share.

16. The Court of Appeal therefore held as follows: Mrs Capehorn was the sole legal and beneficial owner of the farm and the house. Mr Harris had no valid claim to either of those properties. On the other hand, under their agreement Mr Harris was effectively the sole beneficial owner of the shares in the company and Mrs Capehorn no longer had any beneficial interest in those.

17. The reasoning for the decision in *Capehorn v Harris* is fairly straightforward to follow – the first instance judge had erroneously elided between the two stages of analysis and proceeded

to impute the parties' intentions when she had not had cause to do so.

18. It was, perhaps, the ease with which it is possible to discern the two-stage approach in *Capehorn v Harris* and that made the decision of a differently constituted Court of Appeal in *Barnes v Phillips*[19], released just three months later, all the more remarkable.

<u>Barnes v Phillips</u>

19. Like in *Capehorn v Harris*, the parties in *Barnes v Phillips* also began a relationship in 1983, although they began to cohabit in 1989. In 1996, they purchased their first property together, at which time they had had their first child, who was by then two years old. They later had a second child. The property was purchased in their joint names for £135,000, funded by their joint savings of £25,000, and a joint repayment mortgage of about £110,000. The lower court found that at the time of purchase the parties were joint tenants in law and equity as that was their common intention. Mr Barnes paid the mortgage and life insurance, whilst Ms Phillips paid the council tax. They shared the utility bills. Mr Barnes was thought to have made greater financial contributions because he earned more, but Ms Phillips made a greater contribution to the care of their children. In 2005, they separated. Mr Barnes departed. For two and a half years he paid towards the mortgage and he also paid started paying £250 per month towards the children. By 2008, he had stopped paying to the mortgage. Mr Barnes's financial contributions to the children were by this stage sporadic and Ms Phillips's evidence was that she was unable to rely on them. At first instance, the trial judge found that there had been *no* discussions or agreement by the parties after separation to change their otherwise jointly held interest in the property. The judge therefore decided that he would impute an intention for them

19 [2016] 2 FLR 1292

"which the court considers fair, having regard to the whole course of dealing between them in relation to the property[20]". In only the second reported example of the parties' shares altering in a property post separation[21], the trial judge awarded Mr Barnes only a 15% share in a property of which he had started out as the joint legal and equal beneficial owner. A significant part of the reason for this was said to be that, just prior to separation, there had been a re-mortgage of the property, and the trial judge had found that Mr Barnes had had the exclusive benefit of a significant proportion of the re-mortgage monies. A second reason given was that, in the years that followed, Mr Barnes got to the position where he was unable to maintain his own contributions to the monthly mortgage repayments, or to the support of his children[22].

20. The difficulty for the Court of Appeal was that there was <u>no finding</u> by the trial judge that the parties *had intended for their shares to change*, which he could then use as the basis to go on to hold that they could not agree what those shares would be (hence the need to then impute). So not unlike *Capehorn v Harris*[23], the trial judge had proceeded to impute an intention, without having explicitly found at the first stage that the parties had a common intention to do so. What did the Court of Appeal do? Did it overturn the decision as had happened in *Capehorn*? No. Instead, Jones L.J., delivering the Court of Appeal's judgment, perhaps rather generously 'read into' the trial judge's decision, and said this[24]:

---

20 As recounted by the Court of Appeal, see para 16.

21 The other being, obviously, *Jones v Kernott*, ibid.

22 Note the potentially far reaching implication in this case that defaulting in the payment of child support to an ex-partner could be a factor on which a change of intentions could be inferred. It remains whether to be seen whether that fact alone would be sufficient; in *Barnes v Phillips* it was one of many factors.

23 Court of Appeal, Ibid, 2015.

[29] "If I am correct in my reading of paragraphs 37 and 38 of the judgment, the judge has moved directly from considering whether there was an express common intention to vary shares in the property to considering in what shares the parties now hold the property, from concluding that there was "no specific agreement" to considering what intention must be imputed as to the shares. A critical step in the process is simply not addressed in the judgment[25]*. As we have seen, the judge was well aware of the structure laid down in Jones v. Kernott within which the issues should be addressed; he had just set it out in great detail in his judgment. He cannot be taken to have departed from it in the radical manner submitted by the appellant. Moreover, he must have appreciated that there would be no point in discussing the shares in which the property is held following variation if no common intention to vary had been established. In these circumstances, it is at the very least strongly arguable that the judge must be taken to have concluded that there was such a common intention. Nevertheless, this stage of the reasoning is totally absent from his judgment.*

[30] "In these circumstances it is open to this court to consider whether a common intention to vary shares should be inferred in the circumstances of this case. It is clear from the judgments of the majority in Jones v. Kernott that the scope for inference in this context is very extensive indeed. (See in particular Lord Walker and Baroness Hale at [34]: "In this area, as in many others, the scope for inference is wide.") It is also significant that the majority in Jones v. Kernott felt able to draw an inference as to the shares in which the property should be held after the variation.

---

24 *Barnes v Philips*, Ibid, paras 29-31.

25 Author's emphasis.

> *[31] "In the present case the weight of the evidence supports an inference that the parties intended to alter their shares in the property..."*

21. In other words, the Court of Appeal held that although the trial judge did not expressly deal with the parties' intentions in his judgment at the first stage, he *must* have considered it because he had recounted the law extensively in the preceding part of his judgment[26] In effect, they said, even though the judge did not deal with the point directly, it must have been in his mind. Consequently, the outcome was that the Court of Appeal upheld the trial judge's decision and awarded Mr Barnes only a 15% share in the property.

22. One further point of note from *Barnes v Phillips* is that Mr Barnes had waited eight years to bring proceedings against his former cohabitee in respect of their jointly owner property. That raises the interesting question as to whether delay in promulgating a TOLATA claim can have an adverse impact on a claim for a simple order for sale and an equal division of the proceeds thereof? Much would appear to depend on whether the departed party (such as Mr Barnes) ceased to pay towards the joint mortgage or otherwise gives the court cause to find that the parties intended for their shares to vary. It does lead to a question however, as discussed at the outset of this chapter, about where the line is to be drawn between prospective equitable accounting and parties' beneficial shares being capable of changing.

<u>Aspden v Elvy</u>

23. A demonstration of where imputation was used to produce a fair outcome in the domestic context may be found in *Aspden v*

26 As with mathematics, it is not always enough to simply arrive at the correct answer. One should normally show one's workings out. But here the Court of Appeal plainly approved of the outcome and rather exceptionally gave the trial judge the benefit of the doubt.

Elvy[27], a sole name case with unusual facts. The case concerned Mr Aspden's claims for an interest in a property under a constructive trust and/or a proprietary estoppel. The parties met in 1985. In 1986, Mr Aspden purchased Outlaithe Farm for £70,000. It comprised a farmhouse, a number of outbuildings, a derelict barn and 6 acres of land. Mr Aspden was registered as sole proprietor. The parties began to cohabit and had two children together. Miss Elvy ran a cattery and dog kennels from the outbuildings of the farm. Mr Aspden worked as a manager for a business but after suffering a heart attack he ceased to work. The parties separated as a couple on or about Christmas in 1995 after about 10 years together. (There was a dispute about the precise date when they separated.) There were allegations of domestic violence, although no findings were made at trial. Miss Elvy moved a short distance away and began to rent a flat. Mr Aspden remained living at the farmhouse. However, they continued to have contact with each other because Miss Elvy continued to run the cattery and kennels from the outbuildings on Mr Aspen's land. He sent her child support for the children every week, in cash. 10 years later, in January 2006, Mr Aspden transferred the Barn to the Miss Elvy. The circumstances in which he did so were disputed. There was a suggestion that he still harboured hopes to marry Miss Elvy. He was also embroiled at that stage in third party litigation and he feared that if he were to lose that case there could be a charge for legal fees placed over his properties. And so Mr Aspden transferred the barn to Miss Elvy, but not the farmhouse. Mr Aspden remained living at the farmhouse until he sold it in January 2008, and he kept the proceeds of sale. The net proceeds of the sale of the farmhouse were sufficient to discharge his creditors and for Mr Aspden to still receive a significant sum from the proceeds of sale, but apparently not enough to purchase a new property to live in. He then moved into a caravan on part of the land within the curtilage of the barn, which by now he had transferred to Miss Elvy. Relations between the

27 [2012] 2 FLR 807

parties improved somewhat. Steps were then taken to convert Outlaithe Barn into a dwelling house. At trial the parties disputed whether it was a joint enterprise or whether the conversion was by Miss Elvy solely. It was common ground that Mr Aspden did some of the building work personally including using his JCB. He also made a contribution of about £60-70,000 to the works. Mr Aspden's case was that there was a common intention that the parties would marry and cohabit again. Miss Elvy stated that the payments were gifts in recognition of her contributions to the family and in respect of her former interest in Outlaithe Farm, in which she had lived for 10 years and of which Mr Aspden had kept all the proceeds of sale. The converted barn, by the time of the trial, was worth £400,000.

24. Mr Aspden pursued his claim on the basis of a constructive trust and/or a proprietary estoppel. Miss Elvy contended that she was the absolute owner of Outlaithe Barn and denied that any trust or proprietary estoppel arose. As well as being a fascinating (not to mention, messy) set of facts, the court's decision was perhaps the first reported attempt by a deputy High Court judge to summarise a single statement of principles arising from *Stack v Dowden* and *Jones v Kernott*. HHJ Behrens[28], reviewed the case law, and held as follows:

> *[92] The two recent House of Lords/Supreme Court cases of Stack v Dowden [2007] 2 AC 432 and Jones v Kernott [2011] 3 WLR 1121 both deal with a situation where the legal title to the property by two persons. There are however passages in the speeches which refer specifically to the situation where the legal title is vested in one person.*
>
> *93 The Stack v Dowden approach applies in a domestic context where two people buy property together and there is*

28 Sitting as a deputy High Court judge at the Leeds District Registry of the High Court.

no express declaration of trust. As explained in Jones v Kernott the approach may be summarised as follows:

1. *The starting point or presumption is that the parties hold the property as beneficial joint tenants. The presumption is difficult to displace or rebut. It can be rebutted where it is established that the parties actually intended at the time of acquisition of the property to hold in equity otherwise than as joint tenants. Guidance is given in paragraph 69 of the speech of Baroness Hale as to the factors necessary to rebut the presumption.*

2. *At the first stage the intention is to be deduced objectively – it is the intention which was reasonably understood by the other party to be manifested by that other party's words or conduct. If the intention so deduced indicates in what shares the property was to be held the court gives effect to that intention.*

3. *If the intention so deduced does not indicate in what shares the property was to be held then (at this stage) the court is obliged to decide upon their respective entitlement by reference to what is fair having regard to the whole course of dealing in relation to the property*

4. *If the parties' intention changes subsequently the court is obliged to give effect to the changed intention. In such a case the court must first seek to ascertain the changed intention objectively and where possible give effect to that intention. Where that search proves fruitless the court is entitled to decide upon that intention by reference to what is fair.*

25. It is submitted that the above extracts from *Aspden v Elvy* contain a helpful and lucid overview of both of the said leading decisions, encapsulated in a few short and easy to read paragraphs. Obviously, the busy practitioner should always refer to

the ratio decidendi expressed in the leading authorities and great care should be taken not to try to over-simplify the complexity of their principles. There can be no real substitute for Lady Hale and Lord Walker's joint summary of their decision contained in paragraphs 51 and 52 of their judgment in *Jones v Kernott*, but it is submitted that above summary is a helpful one in drawing together that case with *Stack v Dowden*[29].

26. The contentious barn in the case had once been owned by Mr Aspden. The trial judge found that in the first instance Mr Aspden has transferred all his beneficial interest to Miss Elvy when he transferred his legal interest. The case was complicated by the fact that later, when they jointly converted it into a residential dwelling, an implied trust then arose in Mr Aspden's favour, giving him a share once again (albeit only limited one). The judge found that there had not been any express discussions that Mr Aspden should obtain an interest in the barn. But he could not accept that Mr Aspden's significant financial contributions to the conversion were intended to be gifts. Accordingly, the judge inferred that there was a common intention that Mr Aspden should have some interest in the barn. However, it was not possible from the facts to say in what shares the parties had intended for Mr Aspden to have. The judge was not assisted by the lack of evidence of the barn before the conversion.[30] In those circumstances, the judge was driven to impute the quantum of the parties' shares. Following *Jones v Kernott* and *Oxley v Hiscock* the judge held that "*In those circumstances I have to impute an intention by reference to what is fair having regard to the whole course of dealing between the parties.*"[31]

---

29 In lengthier extracts not quoted for reasons of space, but to be found at paragraph 94 of the judgment onwards (just after the quoted extract which *is* set out above) HHJ Behrens also referred to specific parts of Lady Hale's decision in *Stack v Dowden*.

30 The only available valuation to the Court was that which was proximate to the time of the litigation.

31 *Aspden v Elvy*, ibid, para 127.

The valuation of the barn for trial purposes was £400,000. Mr Aspden was found as a fact to have spent £65,000-£70,000 of his own money towards the conversion. The judge decided that "*the appropriate fair assessment of the interest is 25%*" representing a "*fair return for the investment of £65,000 to £70,000 and the work carried out by Mr Aspden in a property now worth £400,000*".

27. In *Aspden v Elvy*, incidentally, the court also had to deal with Mr Aspden's proprietary estoppel claim in the alternative. Although it is beyond the scope of this practical TOLATA guide to go into any great detail about proprietary estoppel, it may be helpful for the reader to note what the judge thought about that aspect of the claim. Having summarised the three ingredients necessary for there to be a successful claim of proprietary estoppel – first, a representation made or assurance given to the claimant; second, reliance by the claimant on the representation or assurance; and, third, some detriment incurred by the claimant as a consequence of that reliance[32] – the judge concluded that this aspect of the claim would likely have led to the *same* result. However, it was unnecessary for the judge to consider it in detail because the constructive trust claim had already succeeded and double recovery arising from the same set of circumstances was of course not possible.[33]

32 See para 98 of HHJ Behren's judgment, quoting from the leading authority on proprietary estoppel: *Thorner v Major* [2009] 1 WLR 776.

33 The judge had earlier correctly reminded himself that in proprietary estoppel claims – once the ingredients are satisfied – the "*task of the court is to do justice*" as between the parties. "*The most essential requirement*" the judge said, "*is that there must be proportionality between the expectation and the detriment.*" - See para 101; and also *Jennings v Rice* [2003] 1 FCR 501. The judge went on to say that: "*In these circumstances it is not necessary to consider in detail the claim based on proprietary estoppel. In my view the result would be the same. There were no express representations but Ms Elvy stood by and encouraged Mr Aspden to carry out the work and invest £65,000 - £70,000 in it knowing, as I infer, that the investments were not intended to be gifts and that Mr Aspden did hope and expect to be able to live in and have an interest in Outlaithe Barn. In those circumstances an equity arises. The valu-*

The investment context

28. For the majority of the period since *Stack v Dowden* was decided by the House of Lords, it has been generally accepted that the legal position with regard to the investment context is different to that of the domestic context. That proposition stems from the decision of the Court of Appeal in *Laskar v Laskar*[34] in 2008. That case saw Lord Neuberger, ever the advocate for the certainty of the resulting trust approach, promoted to be the Master of the Rolls and restored to the Court of Appeal in that capacity, presented with a non-cohabitation TOLATA case from which to consider the position anew.

Laskar v Laskar

29. In *Laskar*, the parties were a mother and her daughter. The mother had been a council tenant with Welwyn Hatfield Council under a secure tenancy. She wished to purchase her property under the right to buy scheme but could not afford to do so on her own. One of her daughters, the appellant, who had previously occupied the property as a child but was by now away at university, agreed to purchase the property with her mother. The gross value of the property was £79,500 but was reduced to £50,085 by virtue of the mother's right to buy discount. The parties paid £3,400 and £3,600 respectively towards the purchase and the mother paid the legal fees and associated costs. The remainder of the purchase price was made up of a mortgage of £43,000 taken out in the parties' joint names. The property was then registered in the parties' joint legal names, and the trial judge made findings that: firstly, there were no discussions between the parties as to the ownership of the

---

ation of the equity requires me to do justice having regard to the proportionality between the expectation and the detriment. I think that a 25% share in Outlaithe Barn satisfies that test" (paragraph 129).

34 [2008] 2 FLR 589

beneficial content in the property; and secondly, that while the appellant daughter was jointly liable on the mortgage, the liability was one which in fact she was never likely to be asked to meet. The latter finding was made on the basis that mother and daughter had formulated a plan to more or less immediately let out the property on a commercial basis. Shortly after purchase this plan was actioned and the mother went to live elsewhere with a different daughter – one would assume to the horror of the Council had they known about the plan, although the judgment is silent about that aspect. Thereafter the mother paid all repairs, handled the rents and the mortgage was paid out of the income received. In 2003 there was a dispute. The daughter brought a claim to attempt to realise an interest in the property and an account of the rental income they had received. At first instance, the trial judge ruled that the appellant daughter had a 4.28% interest purely on the basis of the sum she contributed to the initial purchase (£3,400) and ordered that no account of rent should be made. The daughter appealed. Counsel for the appellant relied heavily on *Stack v Dowden* and the common intention constructive trust. Lord Neuberger rejected that argument outright. His Lordship did not accept that Lady Hale's decision in *Stack*, when addressing what she acknowledged to be a "cohabiting couple's" case[35], should automatically apply to a case of this nature. Although the mother and daughter had a 'familial' relationship, the purpose of the purchase was as an *investment*; and the parties were obviously not in a long-term sexual relationship with children of their own, as was the case in *Stack*. This was therefore an arm's length transaction in a property in which neither of them proposed to live upon completion of it. Lord Neuberger reasoned that:

> *"To my mind it would not be right to apply the reasoning in* Stack v Dowden *to such a case as this, where the parties primarily purchased the property as an investment for rental*

35 Stack v Dowden, ibid, at para 40.

income and capital appreciation, even where their relationship is a familial one."[36]

30. Given the absence of any discussion between the parties, Lord Neuberger fell back on the resulting trust. He used this to allow the appeal in part. In particular, he held that the daughter joining with her mother to apply for the mortgage of £43,000 amounted to a £21,500 contribution by the daughter. Coupled with the daughter's contribution to the deposit of £3,400 her total contribution to the property purchase equated to 33% of the value of the property and consequently Lord Neuberger found her to have a share reflecting the value of that investment on a resulting trust basis. The appellant daughter was however unsuccessful in persuading the court that she should have an equal benefit from her mother's right to buy discount – here Lord Neuberger found that this was an unmatched contribution by the mother, hence her greater than 66% share in the overall outcome.

31. The outcome of *Laskar* proved that the resulting trust was not dead; it is still to be found alive and well in investment context cases. The decision in *Laskar* has been subsequently followed by the lower courts, for example in *Erlam and others v Rahman (A Bankrupt) and others.* [37]

Marr v Collie: Squaring the circle?

32. Notwithstanding what is set out above, the practitioner would be well advised to consider the decision of the Court of Appeal in *Laskar* in light of the 2017 Privy Council decision in *Marr v Collie*[38].

36 Ibid, Paragraph 17,

37 [2016] EWHC 111 (CH); Chief Master Marsh, at para 41.

38 [2017] 2 FLR 674

33. *Marr v Collie* was a UK Privy Council appeal from the Bahamas. It concerned two parties who were in a familial relationship and whom had acquired several properties, some of which were said to be investments. The case provides a useful exposition of the overlap between trusts of land in the family home, and trusts of land in investment properties. Lord Kerr gave the leading judgment, with which all of members of the Privy Council agree. Interestingly, those members included both Lord Neuberger and Lady Hale.

34. The facts were briefly as follows. The parties were Canadian and Bahamian. They had had a 17-year relationship. When the relationship ended, a dispute arose as to the beneficial ownership of some of the properties. The legal title to the contentious properties were held in the parties' joint names, but most of the properties' purchase funds, fees and refurbishment costs were provided by the appellant. The appellant claimed that having provided the purchase monies, and the assets being an investment, he was entitled to the full beneficial interest of the properties. The respondent disagreed. Further, the appellant submitted that he had anticipated that the respondent would make an equal financial contribution to the properties, but that did not occur. The evidence as to intention at first instance was conflicting. The trial judge[39] held that the principle set out in *Stack v Dowden* that a conveyance into joint names indicated legal and beneficial joint tenancy unless the contrary was proved only applied to the domestic consumer context, and relied instead upon *Laskar v Laskar*. He therefore held that it was incorrect to apply the *Stack v Dowden* principle where the primary purpose of the property purchase had been as an investment, even if there was a personal relationship between the parties. He said that the respondent had not rebutted the presumption of a resulting trust.

39 Isaac J. sitting in the High Court of the Bahamas.

35. The Court of Appeal allowed the appeal and found that there was cogent evidence that the parties intended the respondent to have an equal share in the properties. On a further appeal to the Privy Council, Lord Kerr held as follows. First, *Laskar* was not authority for the proposition that the principle in *Stack v Dowden* (that a conveyance into joint names indicated legal and beneficial joint tenancy unless the contrary was proved) applied *only* in the domestic consumer context. Where a property was bought in the joint names of a cohabiting couple, even solely as an investment, it did "*not follow inexorably that the resulting trust solution must provide the inevitable* answer *as to how its beneficial ownership was to be determined.*"[40] It was entirely conceivable, said Lord Kerr, that partners in a relationship would buy, as an investment, property which was conveyed into their joint names with the intention that the beneficial ownership should be shared equally between them, even though they contributed in different shares to the purchase. Where there was evidence to support such a conclusion, it would be both illogical and wrong to impose the resulting trust solution on the subsequent division of property.[41] Lord Kerr added this[42]:

> *"Lord Neuberger of Abbotsbury did not intend to draw a strict line of demarcation between, on the one hand, the purchase of a family home and, on the other, the acquisition of a so-called investment property in whatever circumstances that took place. It is entirely conceivable that partners in a rela-*

40 Lord Kerr, ibid, para 49.

41 If this approach were to be adopted in England and Wales – bearing in mind *Marr v Collie* is strictly speaking a Privy Council decision – one can certainly imagine a position where two cohabitees who jointly own a home together might decide to buy a holiday cottage elsewhere, to be held jointly notwithstanding the fact that they may make unequal contributions to its purchase. Such a property may be used for a mixture of profit (a holiday let), for example, or for the couple's annual holiday. In those circumstances one could certainly see the force of Lord Kerr's opinion.

42 Still at para 49, ibid.

tionship would buy, as an investment, property which is conveyed into their joint names with the intention that the beneficial ownership should be shared equally between them, even though they contributed in different shares to the purchase. Where there is evidence to support such a conclusion, it would be both illogical and wrong to impose the resulting trust solution on the subsequent distribution of the property."

36. Secondly, Lord Kerr held that save where there was no evidence from which the parties' intentions could be identified, the answer was not to be provided by the triumph of one presumption, joint beneficial ownership or a resulting trust, over another. In a section of his judgment entitled "a clash of Presumptions" at paragraphs [53] through to [55], his Lordship said this:

> *[53] "If what Baroness Hale of Richmond described as a 'starting point' (that joint legal ownership should signify joint beneficial ownership) is to be regarded as a presumption, is it in conflict with the presumption of a resulting trust where the parties have contributed unequally to the purchase of property in their joint names? A simplistic answer to that question might be that, if the property is purchased in joint names by parties in a domestic relationship the presumption of joint beneficial ownership applies but if bought in a wholly non-domestic situation it does not. In the latter case, it might be said that the resulting trust presumption obtains."*
>
> *[54] "The Board considers that, save perhaps where there is no evidence from which the parties' intentions can be identified, the answer is not to be provided by the triumph of one presumption over another. In this, as in so many areas of law, context counts for, if not everything, a lot. Context here is set by the parties' common intention – or by the lack of it. If it is the unambiguous mutual wish of the parties, contributing in unequal shares to the purchase of property, that the joint beneficial ownership should reflect their joint legal ownership,*

> *then effect should be given to that wish. If, on the other hand, that is not their wish, or if they have not formed any intention as to beneficial ownership but had, for instance, accepted advice that the property be acquired in joint names, without considering or being aware of the possible consequences of that, the resulting trust solution may provide the answer."*
>
> *[55] "Of course, the initial intention (or lack of it) at the time of purchase may change. This was the reason that the majority in Stack v Dowden emphasised that examination of the course of conduct of the parties over the years in which they dealt with the property is relevant. And it is why an intense examination is warranted of why the properties acquired in this case in 2008 were purchased in joint names. By that time, many of the contributions which, according to Mr Marr, he expected Mr Collie to have made, had not materialised. Why did he continue to agree that the properties should be acquired in joint names?"*[43]

37. Thirdly, Lord Kerr held that given that the intention of the parties was central to the resolution of the issues, the Privy Council felt it had no option but to remit the case to the courts

---

43 It is suggested that the busy practitioner, when analysing all types of cases, should look for emails between the parties to try to decipher their intentions prior to the purchase. In a purely investment context, *Laskar* is still good authority that the shares follow contributions (the resulting trusts approach), since *Marr v Collie* is a Privy Council case and does not overrule *Laskar*. But in a mixed business usage case, the door has always been slightly ajar to the resulting trust given what was said by the Supreme Court in *Jones v Kernott* at para 31 and in *Stack v Dowden* at para 32. Therefore in a case heard in England & Wales with parallel facts to those of *Marr v Collie*, one should be alert to argument in a mixed domestic/business usage case such as the holiday cottage. Text messages or emails demonstrating the parties' true intentions may still prove to be crucial. Remember: "*Context is everything*" (Lady Hale in *Stack v Dowden*). Or, "*if not everything, a lot*" (Lord Kerr in *Marr v Collie*).

below for further consideration. The Judge at first instance had not indicated, had the common intention constructive trust analysis applied, that the result would be the same. Therefore the appeal was allowed and the case was remitted to the Supreme Court of the Bahamas to re-examine the parties' intentions in their 'correct context'.

38. Given that *Marr v Collie* is a relatively recent judgment[44], no general consensus has yet emerged concerning its standing among practitioners. Some may argue that the decision admirably squares the circle between the domestic cohabitation context and the investment context. Given that both Lady Hale and Lord Neuberger sat together in *Marr v Collie* for the first time in a trusts of land case since their divergence of opinion in *Stack v Dowden* ten years previously – and both notably agreed with the reasoning and disposal of the appeal provided by Lord Kerr – to some observers it offers a reconciliation of sorts between their respective viewpoints. After all, what is the purpose of the application of the law of implied trusts if not to give effect to the wishes of the parties? In that regard Lord Kerr was making the point that it would be illogical to impose a solution upon the parties which would have the opposite effect to what they actually intended.

39. The other point of view is that *Marr v Collie* has unintentionally led to more uncertainty, where certainty used to exist. Prior to the decision in *Marr v Collie*, it had been settled law since 2008 that the resulting trust approach shall apply in the investment context[45]. The decision in *Marr v Collie*, although a Privy Council case and therefore not strictly binding upon the Courts of England and Wales[46], has at the very least reignited the

44 At least, at the time of writing this work.

45 See *Laskar v Laskar*, above.

46 Privy Council decisions are persuasive, rather than directly authoritative. (In some circumstances, however, they can be highly persuasive.) Since the

debate about whether the resulting trust should always apply to investment context cases. That may potentially lead in the future to uncertainty concerning the starting point in such a case.

40. There are also other reported examples – beyond the domestic cohabitation context – where the resulting trust presumption may still apply. One instance was in *Ali v Khan* and others[47], where a father transferred legal title of his home to two of his six daughters in order that they might use their borrowing capacity to raise finance to fund their forthcoming marriages. The property had served as a home for the family for many years and at the time of the transfer there were four minor siblings still in occupation. Later, when matters turned sour, one of the two daughters sought possession of the property against her father and mother and asserted that she owned the entirety of the beneficial interest (the second of the daughters had earlier renounced her interest and transferred it to her sister, leaving the first daughter as the sole legal owner and claimant). Their father defended the case, arguing that he had always intended for the vast majority of the beneficial interest to remain his own, save for any part leveraged to pay for the weddings. Although the trial judge found the claimant's position unsatisfactory and opportunistic, he held that there had been, in law, a valid transfer completed in the absence of a formal declaration of

---

Privy Council is "*not a UK court at all, decisions of the Privy Council cannot be binding on any judge of England and Wales, and, in particular, cannot override any decision of a court of England and Wales (let alone a decision of the Supreme Court or the Law Lords) which would otherwise represent a precedent which was binding on that judge*", per Lord Neuberger in *Willers v Joyce &* [2016] UKSC 43, at paragraph 12. However, where there is no inconsistency between the decision of a superior court and the Privy Council, Privy Council decisions will continue to be regarded as being of "great weight and persuasive value" (ibid, same paragraph). The Privy Council can make its own decision binding on the law of England and Wales by directing that it is so.

47 [2002] EWCA Civ 974

trust. The judge concluded that the father had not imposed a written trust obligation on his daughters and that in the absence of a common intention as to how and on what basis the property would be returned to the father in the future, there had been no form of constructive trust by common intention, nor a resulting trust. The trial judge also held that irrespective of the trust issue, the presumption of advancement would have applied as between the father and the claimant daughter, which the father would have been unable to rebut without relying on his own illegality in deceiving the mortgagee into thinking that it had security over the whole property as opposed to only a part.

41. The Court of Appeal overturned the decision, on the following bases. While it accepted that ordinarily the disposal of a legal interest would constitute the disposal of a beneficial interest, it held that extrinsic evidence might be relied on to show the contrary. Further, it held that it was neither unusual nor necessarily improper to transfer the legal estate in land to enable the transferee to raise money on its security.[48] If that had been the true nature of the transaction then the equity of redemption in the property would be held on a resulting trust for the transferor, in this case, the father.[49] But on the facts as found by the trial judge, it had not been the intention of any of the parties that the beneficial interest in the property should have been disposed of by the father. The Court of Appeal gave great weight to the fact that the remainder of the young family still lived there at

48 As to the argument that the father could not rebut the presumption of advancement, had it arisen, without relying on his own fraud or illegality, the Court of Appeal held that there could have been no such deception of the building society unless and until the first defendant had sought to assert priority over his equitable interest over the later legal interest of the building society, and there had been no evidence that he had ever intended to do so, per the Vice Chancellor, Sir Andrew Morritt at para 31.

49 Per the Vice Chancellor, ibid, at para 35. *Haigh v Kaye* (1872) LR 7 Ch 469 and *Re Duke of Marlborough* [1894] 2 Ch 133.

the time of the transfer and continued to do so afterwards. The father paid the household bills both before and after the transfer. There was also no evidence that he wished to give all of his interest in the property to only two of his six children. Accordingly, the Court of Appeal allowed the appeal and held that the father was entitled to the sole beneficial interest in the property, subject to lender's right as first mortgagee. The Court of Appeal suggested that the parties agree directions providing for a re-transfer of legal title back to the father, provided he indemnified the claimant against the mortgage. After all, he had promised to pay for the weddings.

Domestic context with a business element

42. An example of a TOLATA case with a mix of both the domestic and the commercial context is *Geary v Rankine*[50]. In that case, an alleged family partnership dispute saw Mrs Geary bring a claim to be declared, inter alia, the joint beneficiary of a property under a constructive trust. The parties were in a relationship from 1990 to 2009. In the early days of their relationship they lived in London. They had a son together, born in 1992. In 1996 Mr Rankine bought a guesthouse in Hastings in his sole name. He bought it for £61,000, mortgage free, using his own savings. At that stage it was a commercial investment and the parties did not intend to live in it. Mr Rankine initially planned to operate the business himself and to that end he employed a manager. There were then difficulties with the manager. Mr Rankine therefore took over full management of the business himself and moved from London to Hastings in order to do so. For a period, Mrs Geary remained in their London home. After some time, Mr Rankine found he could not cope without some assistance. Mrs Geary moved to Hastings to be with him. She became involved in the running of the business and performed a number of practical and administrative functions. Mr Rankine did not pay Mrs Geary any

50 [2012] 2 FLR 1409

wages. When she wanted money, Mrs Geary would normally have to ask for it. The relationship broke down in 2009. Mrs Geary brought a claim propounded on two arguments. First, she said had an interest in the guesthouse by way of a business partnership. Secondly, in the alternative, she had an interest by virtue of a constructive trust.

43. At trial, the county court judge rejected both of Mrs Geary's claims. Before the Court of Appeal, Mrs Geary pursued both of her original arguments. A strong Court of Appeal[51] rejected both arguments. The Court did not disturb the judge's findings of fact on the nature of the business. They found there had been ample evidence to support the judge's conclusion that there was no business partnership. Even if there had been a partnership, they held, it would not follow that the property was partnership property. A partnership in profits did not indicate that the asset itself was partnership property. One partner might solely own property that the partnership used in its business; and in the instant case the property had been acquired with Mr Rankine's own money before the partnership could have been said to have arisen.

44. As for the constructive trust argument, their Lordships had regard to *Jones v Kernott*[52]. They held that, as the property was titled solely in Mr Rankine's name, Mrs Geary had the burden of establishing a constructive trust. Applying *Jones*, the relevant question was whether there had been a common intention that Mrs Geary would have a beneficial interest in the property. The common intention had to be determined objectively from the parties' conduct and, in this case, although Mrs Geary had presented evidence that the parties had had a common intention to run the business together, it was an impermissible leap to conclude there was a common intention that the property, in which the business had been run, would now belong to both of

51 Comprising Thorpe, L.J., Etherton, L.J., and Lewison, L.J.

52 Ibid, see Chapter 3.

them. Mrs Geary therefore had failed to show that the judge had been wrong in concluding that there had not been a constructive trust.[53] The Court of Appeal also considered whether the parties' intentions had changed over time, pursuant to *Jones v Kernott,* but ultimately upheld the trial judge's findings that they had not[54].

45. *Geary v Rankine* demonstrates the difficulties that claimants in sole names cases may face.[55] In the instant case, Mr Rankine had purchased the contentious property without a mortgage, using all of his own mortgage. He did this at a time when they were already in a relationship. Whatever happened after that Mrs Geary was always going to face an uphill struggle to establish a common intention to share that property.

Bidding for another's share

46. What happens if one co-owner in possession wishes to bid for the other co-owner's share in a jointly owned property? Perhaps the parties have separated and one party wishes to remain at the

---

53 Given that on the evidence Mrs Geary appears to suffer a detriment by working at the property for Mr Rankine for a number of years without any of her own drawings from the business or a formal wage as an employee, one wonders why she did not argue for a proprietary estoppel. Without detailed knowledge of the case, it is difficult to speculate, although one would assume that the simple answer is that Mr Rankine never made such a representation that she would acquire a share; which would be necessary as first of the three ingredients of a proprietary estoppel (the others being 'reliance' and 'detriment').

54 Ibid, para 21

55 There are many other examples of failures to succeed in sole names cases: see *James v Thomas* [2007] EWCA Civ 1212; *Morris v Morris* [2008] EWCA Civ 287; *Thomson v Humphrey* [2009] EWHC 3576 (Ch); and *Dobson v Griffey* [2018] EWHC 1117 (Ch).

property and is confident that they have the funds or the borrowing capacity to purchase the other's share. Can they do it? Can they do it without the other's consent, under court order? Under TOLATA, the court does not, of course, have broad redistributive powers as between co-owners.[56] Under TOLATA, Section 14, the Court may only grant declaratory relief – it can provide clarity as to the parties' respective shares. To be technical, as much of this work makes clear, the court's search is to find the parties' common intention. The Court's power does not extend to substituting its own view for that of the parties. It also cannot force one party to give up or otherwise transfer his or her share to the other. So what, if anything, can be done?

Bagum v Hafiz

47. The answer is to be found in the case of *Bagum v Hafiz*[57]. While the court cannot transfer one party's share to the other, in *Bagum v Hafiz* the Court of Appeal held that it was permissible for a court to order the arrangement of a sale in such a way that one party is entitled to have an opportunity to be the purchaser for the other's share, should that party within a stated time pay an amount determined by a valuation of the property by court order. The lower courts are becoming ever more familiar with this decision – in the author's experience careful drafting of the order is required to remain faithful to the position held by the Court of Appeal, but such an order *is* possible.

48. Strictly speaking, the first instance judge's order, upheld by the Court of Appeal, was that "*there should be a sale of the trust property, preceded by the conferring upon [the Claimant], one of the beneficiaries, of an opportunity to be the purchaser, should he within the stated time pay the amount determined by a valuation*

---

56 As the Court would otherwise have under the Matrimonial Causes Act if the parties had been married.

57 [2016] Ch 241

of the property by the court."[58] Briggs L.J., giving the leading judgment in the Court of Appeal, also added that in "*in many similar cases, the court has ordered a sale of the trust property, with liberty to all beneficiaries to bid, thereby maximising the prospects of the achievement of best value*".[59]

Chaston v Chaston

49. At the time of writing, there is already one reported example of *Bagum v Hafiz* being followed and applied, namely in *Chaston v Chaston*[60]. In that case, there were four children who were all joint executors and equal beneficiaries of their late parents' property. One of the children, Jane, voluntarily sold her share to her brother, John, leaving three of the adult children as beneficial owners (John now having his own 25% share as well as Jane's 25% share for 50% of the total). At first instance, the district judge acceded to John's argument that the property should be sold to him at a price to be determined by a valuation exercise. The other two children had argued that the property be placed on the open market. On appeal, HHJ Paul Matthews sitting as a Deputy High Court dismissed the appeal. He held that the decision of the district judge was one which was open to him, following *Bagum v Hafiz*. Indeed, the effect of the judge's order was for a valuation exercise to determine the market price, and therefore the two appellant siblings were not going to suffer any prejudice by being ordered to sell their shares to their brother.

---

58 Bagum v Hafiz, ibid, at para 26. Briggs L.J. (as he then was) held that such an order by the judge below "fell squarely within her jurisdiction under section 14(2)(a) of TOLATA".

59 Ibid, para 29.

60 [2018] EWHC 1672 (Ch)

CHAPTER FIVE
THE TAKING OF AN ACCOUNT

An overview

1. 'The taking of an account' is typically used to describe the process when, at or near the end of the case, the parties invite the court to adjust the payments to be made to each party from the proceeds of sale in a property. Prior to the coming into force of TOLATA – the statutory machinery of which now governs this process – the fundamental concept was much the same, but derived from equity, hence the label by which this process is more commonly referred to – 'equitable accounting'.

2. The taking of an account, in outline, may be undertaken by way of credits or debits attributable to unmatched mortgage contributions paid by one party but not the other following separation, or by paying other unmatched outgoings necessary to maintain the property after separation, or in consideration of an occupation rent.

3. Equitable accounting must not of course be confused with deciding what the parties' actual beneficial interests are in principle. The Court shall first decide in what beneficial shares the parties hold the property – whether that be in equal or unequal shares. It is also important to note that, absent a change of common intention[1] those shares are absolute and indefeasible and the parties' interests are not liable to be determined, defeated or diminished either automatically or at the court's discretion on the happening of some future event, such as a

1 See Jones v Kernot [2012] AC 776.

separation, per *Turton v Turton*.[2] The court shall always proceed on the basis of the common intention of the parties.[3]

4. After determining the parties' beneficial interests, the court may then be asked to conduct an account – namely to make credits or debits from one party's notional or actual interest in those net proceeds as against the other party, to ensure that a fair outcome is reached regarding the minutiae of expenditure on the property. The account is generally taken of transactions since separation[4].

5. The process of an equitable account by way of court proceedings will only commence once the extent of the parties' beneficial interests has been determined, since the requirement to account (where it exists) reflects and derives from those beneficial interests.[5] For example, if one is only found to have a 10% beneficial interest in a property to the other party's 90% share, (absent any other agreement) it would hardly be fair for that person to be asked to pay 50% of the costs of maintaining it.

---

2 [1988] Ch 542, Court of Appeal; and see also *Gordon v Douce* [1983] 2 All ER 228 and *Walker v Hall* [1984] FLR 126. Indeed, the Court in *Turton v Turton* looked closely at the previous decisions in *Gordon v Douce* and *Walker v Hall* and concluded that on a correct interpretation of the decisions in those cases, it could not be said the court had a discretion as to when to value the parties' interests.

3 It is worth noting that in *Turton v Turton* (Ibid), the gap between separation and the claim by Mrs Turton to realise her half share was eight years, meaning that the potential for passive or negative economic growth many cases could be significant.

4 But this is not an absolute rule: see below in this Chapter.

5 *Wilcox v Tait*, [2007] 2 FLR 871, *Court of Appeal*, per Jonathan Parker L.J., at para [64].

By what process does one take an equitable account?

6. Historically, a taking of an account derived from equitable principles and a body of case law. Following *Stack v Dowden*, it is now clear that the statutory powers of TOLATA "*replaced the old doctrines of equitable accounting*"[6] under which a beneficiary who remained in occupation might be required to pay an occupation rent to a beneficiary who was excluded from the property.

7. Accordingly, "*the criteria laid down in the statute should be applied rather than in the cases decided under the old law, although the results may often be the same*". [7]

8. That does not mean that the body of case law prior to 1997 will cease to be relevant. Indeed, there are many points within them that provide a ready answer or guidance for cases which arise post 1997. But the starting point shall now always be the machinery of the Act, as to which, see Chapter 2.

9. An equitable account may take place in both Part 7 and Part 8 claims, and it will typically be dealt with at the end of a case, usually after the property had been sold and the actual net proceeds of sale are known to the parties and the court.[8]

10. Let us examine a simple scenario of how to take an account. In this example, a property is held by two parties in equal shares and the net value of the property after redemption of the

---

6 These are the words of Lady Hale at para [94] of *Stack v Dowden*, Ibid.

7 Lady Hale at [94] of *Stack v Dowden*, Ibid. See Chapter 2 for the relevant parts of TOLATA itself, sections 12, 13, 14 and 15.

8 per *Wilcox v Tait*, ibid, Court of Appeal, but note that a different approach was taken in *Young v Lauretani* [2007] 2 FLR 1211 (High Court) where a Chancery Division Judge permitted an account prior to a sale, because each party wished to bid for the other's share without a sale to a third party, but could not be sure that they could afford it unless and until an account was taken.

mortgage and costs of sale is a round £300,000. To make it easy, let us say the parties both continued to occupy the property after the end of their relationship up until the sale, albeit in separate bedrooms. The monthly mortgage repayments were £1,000 until sale. The annual buildings insurance was £500. There is no question of an occupation rent arising because they both occupy the property. However, from the point of separation, one party (let us call him Ross) stops paying his half share of the monthly mortgage payments, and the other party (let us call her Rachael) is forced to pay both parties' contributions to avoid going into mortgage arrears and affecting her credit rating. Ross does, however, renew the annual buildings insurance premium at a cost of £500 of which Rachael fails to reimburse him her half contribution, despite his demand. The property then takes 14 months to sell from the date of separation.

Fig.1 – Declaration of the Court

Rachael's Beneficial share	**Ross' Beneficial Share**
50% = £150,000	50% = £150,000

Fig.2 – Example showing the process at an equitable account hearing

Rachael's Beneficial share	Ross' Beneficial Share
50%	50%
= £150,000 (in principle)	= £150,000 (in principle)
Credit: £7,000 due from Ross to Rachael because Ross did not pay his half of the joint monthly mortgage repayments from the breakdown of the relationship until sale	Debit: £7,000 due to Rachael from Ross because Ross did not pay his half of the joint monthly mortgage repayments from the breakdown of the relationship until sale
14 x £500 = +£7,000	14 x £500 = -£7,000
Debit: £250 being half of the cost of the buildings insurance not paid by C when D renewed it between separation and sale.	Credit: £250 being half of the cost of the buildings insurance not paid by C when D renewed it between separation and sale.
-£250	+£250
Final Account:	Final Account:
£150,000 +£7,000 -£250 = £156,750	£150,000 -£7,000 +£250 = £143,250

11. Accordingly, one can see that the parties would have been entitled to £150,000 of the net proceeds of sale in principle but following an equitable account the actual division of the proceeds of sale will be divided so as to give credit for the net contributions made by Rachael.

12. Now, again using the above example, imagine that Rachael, as the Claimant, had made a Part 36 offer, before any proceedings had started, offering to accept a simple sale of the property and for both parties to take an equal share of the proceeds of sale and offering to forgo her claim for an equitable account regarding Ross' unpaid mortgage contributions. Suppose Ross refused that offer or otherwise ignored it. In the above example – assuming the court had declared that Rachael had a 50% beneficial interest (which was, in fact, common ground), had ordered a sale, and at the taking of the account hearing had ordered a division on an account as set out in Fig. 2 above – Rachael would be entitled to argue that she has beaten her Part 36 offer. She would therefore be likely entitled to the costs consequences following judgment of CPR 36.17. The cost consequences for Ross will therefore be very severe.

From when does an equitable account start to run?

13. The time from which a taking of an account starts to run may be different in every case, because it will be subject to the common intentions of the parties.[9] In a cohabitation case, however, it is likely that the parties would not intend for an account to start to run prior to the breakdown of their relationship. Consequently, in *Clarke v Harlowe*[10], it was held that in an ordinary case of cohabitation, equitable accounting will begin at the date of separation because, in general, payment for

---

9 *Wilcox v Tait* [2006] EWCA Civ 1867, per Jonathan Parker L.J., at para [65].

10 [2007] 1 FLR 1

outgoings or improvements prior to the date of separation would likely be in accordance with the arrangements between the parties and the common purpose of the implied trust under which the property was held. In that case, the court observed that, ordinarily, the common purpose of the trust would subsist while the relationship subsisted. After the relationship ended and the parties separated, the common purpose of the implied trust would generally come to an end, and no common arrangements between the parties would survive, so that each ought to discharge his or her proportionate share of the outgoings, with appropriate accounting on the sale of the property in the event of any failure to honour that obligation.

14. However, in a case which concerns a commercial investment, where each of the parties has agreed to pay one half of the monthly mortgage repayments in pursuit of a joint investment, a taking of an account could well extend into the period during which the parties were in a relationship.[11] There are even examples of reported cases where, in a cohabitation case, the accounting exercise could run during the period when the relationship was still subsisting, for example in *Marsh v von Sternberg*[12], when the Court found that where the parties had specifically agreed to pay half each of the monthly mortgage repayments during their relationship, and one party failed to do so, that could be accounted afterwards, even though they had been in a relationship at the time. Accordingly, it should be stressed that the common intentions of the parties in any individual case are crucial to determining the date from which an

11 This point was made, obiter, by the judge in *Clarke v Harlow* (HHJ Behrens sitting as a Deputy HCJ), at paragraph [33]. In a later case before the same judge, *Ketteringham v Hardy* [2011] EWHC 162 (Ch), HHJ Behrens was fortified in the views he had expressed in *Clarke v Harlowe* by the fact that the Court of Appeal in *Wilcox v Tait* (ibid) cited that judgment with approval.

12 [1986] 1 FLR 526, per Bush J. at 534.

equitable may start to run.[13] As the Court of Appeal concluded in *Wilcox v Tait*: "*in an ordinary cohabitation case equitable accounting is only likely to come into play in respect of the period following the termination of the relationship between the co-owners. However, there can be no absolute rule as to that*"[14].

In what circumstances does an occupation rent normally arise?

15. In *Stack v Dowden*, Mr Stack left the contentious property voluntarily following Family Law Act 1996 proceedings. By a consent order, he agreed to depart his home of nine years on the basis of a time limited order (nine months) which provided for his exclusion, but which required Ms Dowden to pay him a sum which reflected the cost of his alternative accommodation, later agreed at £900 per month. If she could not pay him monthly from her income, she agreed to pay from her share of the proceeds of sale in due course. After that order expired, Mr Stack did not return to the property, but had to pay for his alternative accommodation without the benefit of the £900 per month credit.

16. In the TOLATA proceedings, Mr Stack therefore claimed for an occupation rent for the period from which the Family Law Act order expired. The trial judge made that order on the sole stated ground that Ms Dowden had control over the marketing and sale of the house. The Court of Appeal thought this reason unsatisfactory, and reversed that decision, on the grounds that

13 See, for example, Jonathan Parker L.J. in Wilcox v Tait, Ibid, at para [66], where his Lordship said: "*I agree with Judge Behrens in Clarke v Harlowe that in the ordinary cohabitation case it is open to the court to infer from the fact of cohabitation that during the period of cohabitation it was the common intention of the parties that neither should thereafter have to account to the other in respect of expenditure incurred by the other on the property during that period for their joint benefit. Whether the court draws that inference in the given case* will of course depend on the facts of that case*. (*author's emphasis).

14 Ibid, per Jonathan Parker L.J., at para [74].

the house was soon to be sold, the children of the parties were living there, and there was no basis for assessing the compensation at £900 per month. Lady Hale upheld that part of the Court of Appeal's decision in her leading judgment when the appeal came before to the House of Lords.[15] It should be noted however that Lady Hale had regard to the fact that it had been agreed that the property should be sold as soon as possible, so it had been intended that he should not have been kept out of his money for very long.[16]

17. Lord Neuberger, in a minority of one in that case, would have allowed an occupation rent. He considered the interplay between the various sections of TOLATA namely sections 12, 13 and 15.[17] He held that after the Family Law Act order had expired, the decision as to whether to require Ms Dowden to pay occupation rent to Mr Stack was a matter for the court. Lord Neuberger would have held that it was right to order compensation to be paid. He noted that Mr Stack was paying the meet his rental accommodation expenses. The jointly owned property was by now mortgage free, albeit that it housed the parties' children and Ms Dowden met the outgoings. Lord Neuberger did not see the occupation by the children as a factor not to pay an occupation rent – there was no prejudice to them, he said, by Ms Dowden being ordered to give Mr Stack a credit on the eventual sale.

18. So, a voluntary departure (on terms) may or may not give rise to an occupation rent, depending on the circumstances. Does a simple and completely voluntary departure (without agreed terms) give rise to an occupation rent? The answer would appear to depend on the facts of the case. It is certainly now clear that there need not be any forcible ouster from the property for an

15 *Stack v Dowden*, per Lady Hale, at para [94].

16 Ibid, also at para [94].

17 *Stack v Dowden*, ibid, per Lord Neuberger at paras [150] – [153].

occupation rent to arise in principle. In *Murphy v Gooch*[18], the Court of Appeal held that credit may be given by way of an occupation rent if it is "just" to do so, whether or not there was proof of actual ouster. In that case, on the breakdown of the parties' relationship, Ms Murphy left the property with the parties' daughter, to live elsewhere. Mr Gooch remained in the property. There was no suggestion that there had been any violence or unsatisfactory conduct on the part of Mr Gooch whatsoever, but the Court of Appeal agreed that given the breakdown of the parties' relationship, Ms Murphy should be regarded as "*constructively excluded*"[19]. Further, in *Amin and another v Amin and others*,[20] Warren J., sitting in the Chancery Division, held that a person's entitlement to occupy was not only to be excluded by "*actual physical exclusion or a demand by the trustees to vacate*[21]". He continued: "If a person is effectively excluded by threat or unpleasantness, that must surely qualify as exclusion. It will be a matter of fact and degree in any particular case whether there has been exclusion within the statutory sense."

19. But take another example. Suppose two co-owners separate and one decides to emigrate, or to spend some years travelling the world, leaving no forwarding address and making no offer to contribute to the outgoings on the property, however minimal. In those circumstances the court may well decide that it would not be just for the remaining party and co-trustee to begin to accrue an occupation rent liability in favour of their departed former cohabitee[22]. But suppose instead the departed co-owner

18 [2007] EWCA Civ 603.

19 Ibid., per Lightman J., at para [18].

20 [2009] EWHC 3356 (Ch),

21 Ibid, at para [289].

22 The above scenario is a hypothetical example. But in Dennis v McDonald [1982] Fam 63 at 70 to 71, Purchas J., held that: "*...only in cases where the tenants in common not in occupation were in a position to enjoy their right to occupy but chose not to do so voluntarily, and were not excluded by any relevant*

relocates to rented property in the vicinity of the property (the 'just around the corner' example) – and has to pay a great deal of rent in order to meet his or her housing needs. In those circumstances the court may very well think it is appropriate for the remaining co-owner to pay an occupation rent for the benefit of living at the property[23]. As was held by the Court of Appeal in *Murphy v Gooch,* the task of the court is "*to do justice between the parties with due regard to the relevant statutory considerations.*"[24]

20. It has further been held that a beneficiary of a trust does not necessarily need a right to occupy a trust property in order for the right to an occupation rent to arise. In *French v Barcham*[25], the High Court held that where one of the joint owners had gone bankrupt and his affairs were managed by his trustee in bankruptcy – and the trustee had no right to occupy the property under the provisions of the Act – it was nevertheless fair for the remaining owner to pay the trustee in bankruptcy an occupation rent under equitable accounting principles. Blackburne J. held that if there was some reason why the co-owner was not in occupation and it would be unreasonable, looking at the matter practically, to expect that co-owner to take occupation of the property in question, it would normally be fair

---

factor, would the tenant in common in occupation be entitled to do so free of liability to pay an occupation rent." (author's emphasis). Dennis v McDonald concerned a cohabiting couple whose relationship had broken down. There had been domestic violence. Purchas J. had no hesitation in ordering an occupation rent on the basis that "*whatever might have been the cause of the breakdown of the association, it would be quite unreasonable to expect the plaintiff to exercise her rights as a tenant in common to occupy the property as she had done before the breakdown of her association with the defendant.*" His decision on that point was not disturbed on appeal.

23 Subject of course to any offset for paying the mortgage (see below).

24 Ibid, per Lightman J., at para [18]

25 [2008] EWHC 1505

and equitable to charge the occupying co-owner an occupation rent. Blackburne J. did however add that:

> "*if it could be shown that the occupying co-owner was given by the trustee to understand that no occupation rent would be charged or was unaware of, and had no reasonable means of discovering, the other co-owner's bankruptcy, the court might take the view that it would not be just to require the occupying co-owner to pay an occupation rent. But short of such circumstances it is difficult to see why the occupying co-owner should not be charged an occupation rent.*"[26]

21. Ultimately, consideration of an occupation rent is a discretionary exercise, which now involves applying the machinery of TOLATA to the facts of each case. But, as Lord Neuberger observed, cases which pre-date TOLATA may still be useful. To that end, the words of Millet J. in *Re Pavlou*[27] are both well-known and extremely persuasive, having been cited with approval in many cases since TOLATA came into force.[28] In that case, Millet J. said this:

> "*I take the law to be to the following effect. First, a court of equity will order an inquiry and payment of occupation rent, not only in the case where the co-owner in occupation has*

26 However it should be noted that Blackburne J's approach in *French v Barcham* was doubted by another judge of the Chancery Division in the more recent case of *Davis v Jackson and another* [2017] 1 WLR 4005, which should therefore be carefully analysed. In the latter case, Snowden J was unconvinced by Blackburne J's reasoning, and did not order the bankrupt's spouse to pay occupation rent to the trustee in bankruptcy. Snowden J. did however say that his own decision was specific to the facts of that case, bearing in mind the court has a broad equitable jurisdiction to do justice between co-owners. Given the divergence of opinion, however, it may be that this point requires to be further tested before the Court of Appeal.

27 [1993] 1 WLR 1046 at 1050 C-D

28 Including *Wilcox v Tait*, ibid.

ousted the other, but in any other case in which it is necessary in order to do equity between the parties that an occupation rent should be paid. The fact that there has not been an ouster or forceful exclusion therefore is far from conclusive. Secondly, where it is a matrimonial home and the marriage has broken down, the party who leaves the property will, in most cases, be regarded as excluded from the family home, so that an occupation rent should be paid by the co-owner who remains. But that is not a rule of law; that is merely a statement of the prima facie conclusion to be drawn from the facts. The true position is that if a tenant in common leaves the property voluntarily, but would be welcome back and would be in a position to enjoy his or her right to occupy, it would normally not be fair or equitable to the remaining tenant in common to charge him or her with an occupation rent which he or she never expected to pay."

22. A more subtle example of a tricky occupation rent issue is one where a departed co-owner leaves behind a locked former bedroom which still contains their personal belongings, on the basis that they would be back to collect them but never did. Suppose in this example the parties are both siblings and joint beneficiaries of a trust property left to them by their parents. They have a strained relationship. The remaining co-owner could reasonably argue that the departed co-owner has had exclusive use of his or her bedroom, which they chose not to occupy and thereby deprived the remaining co-owner of the use of that part of the property. On the other hand, the departed co-owner might say that they could not live with their sibling and that *they* should receive an occupation rent for being deprived of the use of the majority of the property, to which the remaining co-owner would argue they did not prevent the other from living there. The resolution of an issue such as this would depend on the facts of the case, and whether the court finds that departed co-owner would be 'welcome back' as Millet J. put it

in *Re Pavlou*[29], or is instead being constructively excluded, as was the case in *Murphy v Gooch*[30].

How does one quantify an occupation rent?

23. In *Stack v Dowden*, Lord Neuberger gave the only real analysis in the House of Lords as to how one may quantify an occupation rent. In his view, the occupation rent is to be "*often*" calculated "*on the basis of the rental value of the trust property concerned*".[31] But in *Stack v Dowden*, the figure that Lord Neuberger would have awarded was based on Mr Stack's costs of living elsewhere. He said, at Paragraph 157:

> *"I also disagree with the Court of Appeal on quantum. I can see no reason to depart from the figure which the parties originally agreed, and was not challenged before the Judge, namely £900 per month. It is a figure which had a rational basis (namely the cost of Mr Stack's alternative accommodation). There is, in my view, a strong argument for saying that, on the basis of an analogy with trespass damages, that the court should be able to award compensation based either on the notional rental value of the house or the cost of the alternative accommodation."*

---

29 Ibid.

30 Ibid.

31 *Stack v Dowden*, ibid, per Lord Neuberger at para [154]. See also *Leigh v. Dickeson* (1884) 15 Q.B.D. 60, where one tenant in common leased his interest to his co-tenant in common, giving that latter exclusive possession of the property. When the lease expired, the co-tenant remained in occupation. The Court of Appeal held that, on the facts of that case, the occupier was to be considered as holding exclusive possession of the house upon the terms of the lease, and therefore, he was liable for rent to his co-owner at the same rate as was reserved by the lease, in other words, the market rent.

24. It should be noted, of course, that this was a minority opinion in that case. But it is likely to be of great persuasive value in many subsequent cases, not least because of the stature of the judge providing it, and the lack of any detailed analysis of this issue by any of the other members of the Appellate Committee (who simply agreed with the Court of Appeal not to order an occupation rent on the facts of that case). And while we must remember to be cautious about our treatment of equitable accounting cases which pre-date the coming into force of TOLATA, Lord Neuberger has himself observed[32] that it will be a rare case where the statutory principles would produce a different result from that which would have resulted from the equitable principles. It may therefore be of assistance that in *Dennis v. McDonald*[33], the Court of Appeal held that the correct quantum of occupation rent should be the same as the fair rent that would have applied at that time under the Rent Act 1977. Given that there are few remaining Rent Act tenancies remaining – as all new private sector tenancies are generally assured shorthold tenancies – it is arguable that in the modern context *Dennis v McDonald* could be interpreted to mean the reasonable market rent.

Will the quantum of the occupation rent be proportionate to the number of co-owners?

25. Yes. In Aktar v Hussain[34], the Court of Appeal held that a judge had erred by not allowing a 50% discount to the market occupation rent claimed, when the party in occupation of the property was a 50% co-owner of that property.

---

32 *Stack v Dowden*, ibid, per Lord Neuberger at para [150].

33 [1982] Fam. 63

34 [2012] EWCA Civ 1762

26. However, where the house is an "open house", available to a class of beneficiaries who have not reached any common intention as to their regulation of the living arrangements of the property, an occupation rent may not be payable. In *M'Mahon v Burchell*[35] a father left his property to his seven adult children as tenants in common – of whom one occupied it full time, three occasionally occupied it, and the remaining three did not occupy it at all. William, the party who occupied it full time was held to be not liable to the others for occupation rent in respect of his occupation, because where there was no contract or exclusion, occupation by one tenant in common created no liability for rent to the other tenants in common.

Do unmatched mortgage repayments offset an occupation rent, and if so, need they be capital repayment or interest only?

27. Typically, yes, and the general consensus of the authorities[36] is that they need only be interest only to offset a claim for occupation rent. However, this should not be treated as an absolute rule of law because the authorities make clear that each case will be fact specific. In any event a taking of an account is discretionary; the court will be concerned to achieve a just outcome. Who better to define the issue at hand than Lord Denning M.R., who set out the conundrum in his usual inimitable style in *Bernard v. Josephs.*[37] Lord Denning put it thus:

> *"After ascertaining the shares, the next problem arises when it is to be turned into money. Usually one of the parties stays in*

35 *(1846) 1 Coop t Cott 457 (47 ER 944)*

36 It is hard to discern an absolute rule, because the authorities themselves point out that all cases are both discretionary and fact specific, but see for example: *Bernard v. Josephs* [1982] Ch. 391, at 400; *Re Gorman (a bankrupt)*, ibid; *Re Pavlou*, ibid; *Leake v Bruzzi* [1974] 1 WLR 1528; and *Byford v Butler*, ibid.

37 [1982] Ch. 391, at 400.

the house, paying the mortgage instalments and the rates and other outgoings. The house also increases in value greatly owing to inflation. None of that alters the shares of the parties in the house itself. But it does mean that when the house is sold - or the one buys the other out - there have to be many adjustments made. The value of the house itself is taken at the value at the time of sale or buying out. There must be deducted from it all the money needed to redeem the mortgage. Then the one in possession must be given credit for paying the other's share of the mortgage instalments and be debited with an occupation rent for using the other's share of the house. Other adjustments may be needed for other outgoings. Then the net amount must be divided according to the shares.

28. In *Bernard v Josephs*, by the time of the appeal before Lord Denning, Miss Bernard had been living away from the house for five years, while Mr Josephs had remained together with – for a large part of that time – a new wife. During Mr Josephs' and Miss Bernard's relationship they had sub-let parts of their house to tenants, and this practice had apparently continued after Miss Bernard's departure. Lord Denning said:

> *"...Seeing that he has the use of her share, it would only be fair that he should pay an occupation rent in respect of it: see* Dennis v. McDonald *[1982] Fam. 63, 64. No doubt, however, he has been paying the whole of the mortgage instalments and this should be taken into account as well. It may relieve him of paying any occupation rent for her half-share."*

29. Lord Denning's solution was to:

> *"...deduct one-half of the amount paid by Mr. Josephs since the separation for mortgage instalments (deducting, of course, the amount received from the tenants). He should only get*

> *credit for one-half, because he has had the benefit of her half-share. Then make any other special adjustments."*[38]

30. It should be noted, for completeness, that Lord Denning was minded not to force Mr Josephs to leave the property given that he had been settled in it with his new wife for three years, so long as Miss Bernard was not to be treated unfairly. Therefore Lord Denning made an order for sale of the property, but not to be enforced provided that within four months Mr Josephs could pay Miss Bernard a sum reflecting the total value of her beneficial interest in the property[39] (at the up to date value with vacant possession), subject to the accounting exercise set out above.

31. *Bernard v Joseph* was followed in *Re Gorman (a bankrupt),*[40]. In that case, the husband had left the home, having become bankrupt. Vinelott J., giving the judgment of the Divisional Court of the Chancery Division, held that that the wife (who had continued to pay the mortgage capital and interest repayments in his absence) should be entitled to credit for her payments to the mortgage capital but should only be entitled to credit for the payment of mortgage interest if there was a set off for a notional occupational rent against the mortgage interest payments. His Lordship said this[41]:

> *"In some cases, to avoid the necessity of expensive and protracted inquiries and accounts, the courts have treated mortgage interest, paid by a tenant in common who has been in sole occupation, as equal to an occupation rent, leaving only an appropriate proportion of any capital repayments to*

---

38 Ibid, at 401.

39 Which provides an interesting background context to the more recent case of *Bagum v Hafiz* [2016] Ch 241 (see Chapter 3)

40 [1990] 1 WLR 616

41 Ibid, at P.625

be credited to him. That was the course taken in Suttill v. Graham [1977] 1 W.L.R. 819. Stamp L.J., after referring to the principles laid down in Pettitt v. Pettitt *[1970] A.C. 777, and* Gissing v. Gissing *[1971] A.C. 886, said, at pp. 821–822:*

"applying those principles a beneficiary entitled to an equal share in equity of property of which he is a trustee, and which he himself occupied, is to be charged with at least an occupation rent; so that if as here he seeks to charge his co-beneficiary trustee with half the outgoings, he should be charged with half the occupation rent. That is not precisely the way in which such a situation has been [1990] 1 WLR 616 at 626 approached in the cases to which attention has been called by counsel on behalf of the husband. But in Leake (formerly Bruzzi) v. Bruzzi [1974] 1 W.L.R. 1528 this court arrived at a similar conclusion by regarding the mortgage interest paid by the husband while in possession as something equivalent to rent or payment for use and occupation. That will normally produce a fair result and save costs; and where, as here, the husband in possession does not submit to be charged with an occupation rent, it must be wrong that he should seek to charge the wife with half the mortgage interest which he has paid while living in the property rent free and resisting a sale of the property.

32. The reader should note that Vinelott J. and Stamp L.J. respectively made the point in each appeal that the set off is a *convenient mechanism* to avoid the necessity of expensive and protracted inquiries, which will normally produce a fair result and save costs. It remains to be seen whether, at a time when interest rates have been exceptionally low for a long period, the Courts will continue in the future to treat it as fair that the party remaining in occupation may be entitled to offset a claim for occupation rent but making relatively meagre interest only

mortgage repayments, when compared against a much higher monthly rental payment for the departed party.[42]

33. *Leake v Bruzzi*[43], referred to by Stamp L.J. in *Suttill v. Graham* above, is another example where a claim for occupation rent was offset against the interest element of the mortgage only. After the wife departed the family home, the husband alone repaid the full monthly mortgage instalments and had sole occupation of the former matrimonial home. The Court of Appeal held that after the separation he was entitled to credit from the wife for half the capital repayments he had made under the mortgage, in conjunction with the fact that the payments of mortgage interest which he had made could be regarded as the equivalent of payment for his use and occupation of the property.[44]

34. Further, in *Byford v Butler*[45], a husband was made bankrupt but continued to live with his wife in their matrimonial home for a further ten years before he passed away. The trustee in bankruptcy, who was the Official Receiver, did nothing during the husband's lifetime. After his death, the wife offered to purchase the trustee's share, which was rejected, and a dispute arose about the mortgage interest repayments which the wife had made

42 In this regard, a modern test case would be welcome. Most of the authorities concerning the policy of set-off between the payment of the interest only part of a mortgage and a claim for occupation rent date back to a time when interest rates were higher. Why is it fair, one might argue, for there to still be a policy of set-off when the cost of paying the interest only mortgage on a favourable tracker mortgage product in an age of ultra-low interest rates is vastly more advantageous to paying a private sector market rent for a similar sized property in the same area?

43 [1974] 1 WLR 1528

44 *Leake v Bruzzi* [1974] 1 WLR 1528, at 1532/3 per Ormrod L.J. at 1533H. Although this was a claim under Section 17 of the Married Woman's Property Act, it was held in *Dennis v McDonald* [1981] 2 All ER 632 (Court of Appeal) to be a sound authority for equitable accounting cases under other property statutes.

45 [2004] 1 FLR 56.

alone in the intervening period during which the property had gone up in value. During the proceedings, the wife sought an account for the mortgage interest payments she had made, and in response the trustee in bankruptcy sought an occupation rent as against the wife, but offered to offset the one against the other. Laurence Collins J., sitting in the Chancery Division, held on appeal that the wife could only claim credit for mortgage interest payments if there was a set off for occupational rent.

What about other expenses, such as repairs or renovations?

35. It depends on whether the repairs or renovations were consensual. A co-owner has no absolute right to compel another co-owner to indemnify them for works done which the latter had no say over. In *Leigh v Dickeson* (1884) 15 QBD 60, Brett M.R. held that:

> *"The cost of the repairs to the house was a voluntary payment by the defendant, partly for the benefit of himself and partly for the benefit of his co-owner; but the co-owner cannot reject the benefit of the repairs, and if she is held to be liable for a proportionate share of the cost, the defendant will get the advantage of the repairs without allowing his co-owner any liberty to decide whether she will refuse or adopt them.... No such claim as that put forward in the present counter-claim can be found to have been upheld either at law or in equity. If the law were otherwise, a part-owner might be compelled to incur expense against his will: a house might be situate in a decaying borough, and it might be thought by one co-owner that it would be better not to repair it. The refusal of a tenant in common to bear any part of the cost of proper repair may be unreasonable: nevertheless, the law allows him to refuse, and no action will lie against him."*[46]

46 At page 64-65.

36. In *Re Pavlou*,[47] Millet J. (as he then was) followed *Leigh v Dickeson* and held that the guiding principle was that *"neither party could take the benefit of an increase in the value of the property without making an allowance for what had been expended by the other in order to obtain it"*. It would therefore appear to be a matter of election. If a tenant who was not asked to and did not contribute to the cost of repairs or renovations which enhanced the equity of the property seeks to take a benefit from the other's costs of doing so, it would only be fair that they should make a contribution proportionate to their share in the property. This principle may apply whether the tenants were tenants in common or joint tenants, save that in the case of joint tenants the question would only appear to arise on severance of their joint interest.[48] Millet J. drew a parallel with the position where one party alone makes capital repayments to the mortgage which benefit both parties, where in that instance a proportionate credit would be justified. Nevertheless, evidence that the repairs or renovations enhanced the equity of redemption[49] in the property must be proven.[50]

---

47 Ibid, at P. 1048.

48 Ibid, Millet J. at 1048.

49 In other words, the net value available to the parties on sale.

50 Millet J in Re Pavlou again, ibid, at 1049, where his Lordship said: "*There has to be an inquiry as to the amount expended and the increase, if any, in the value of the property thereby realised. Much expenditure on property is not reflected in any increase in value, and most expenditure on property results in a much smaller increase in value than the amount expended.*" The same requirement for the enhancement of value to be proven was stipulated in *Dennis v McDonald* [1982] 1 All ER 590, where the Court of Appeal had no evidence before it of enhancement, but ordered that if such evidence could be produced for the taking of an account hearing, a credit would be payable. For an example of a case where the Court refused to give credit for repairs because there was no evidence they had enhanced the property's value, see *Davis v Jackson and Another* [2017] 2 FLR 1153,

37. It should be noted however, that none of these older authorities have been fully tested in light of *Jones v Kernott*, and it is conceivable that following *Jones* the facts of certain cases may give rise to argument about whether an expenditure by a remaining party to the disinterest of the other could start to provide the basis to infer a change of common intention as to their beneficial interests.

CHAPTER SIX
ESSENTIAL PROCEDURE

Part I: The interplay between TOLATA claims and family proceedings

1. Given that the reader of this work may be either a family lawyer or a litigation lawyer, it may be helpful to explain (i) the essential family and civil procedure that may apply; and (ii) the position where TOLATA issues arise in family law proceedings, most frequently as a trial of a preliminary issue in order to determine the extent of the assets available for division by the family court.

2. In terms of the civil procedure, Part II of this Chapter sets out an overview of the Civil Procedure Rules 1998 (as amended) which most likely to be relevant to managing a TOLATA claim in the High Court or the County Court.

Joinder and trials of TOLATA preliminary issues

3. In the case of family procedure, including a trial of a preliminary issue, the position is as follows. Where a third party claims into, or is otherwise joined to, existing family law proceedings – say, for a trial as a preliminary issue as to whether or not that third party is the beneficial owner of property held by a spouse within financial remedy proceedings under the Matrimonial Causes Act 1973 – it will almost certainly be the case that the Family Procedure Rules 2010 shall apply[1]. Whatever procedure rules are treated by the court as applicable, it is important to

---

1 It has been well established since *Tebbutt v Haynes* [1981] 2 All ER 238 (per Lord Denning M.R. at 241) that a dispute between a spouse and a third party as to the beneficial ownership of property can be adjudicated in ancillary relief proceedings.

remember that the Act and the principles of case law described in this book apply equally to both types of cases.

4. In intervenor claims, the practitioner should particularly note two important decisions: *TL v ML (Ancillary Relief: Claim Against Assets of Extended Family)* [2006] 1 FLR 1263 and *Fisher Meredith v JH and PH* (Financial Remedy: Appeal: Wasted Costs) [2012] 2 FLR 536. Both are decisions of Mostyn J., although in the earlier case of *TL v ML* he was sitting in his then capacity as a deputy High Court Judge.

5. *TL v ML* is the family law authority which, amongst other things, sets out the principles which shall apply to the joinder of a third party, such as to determine whether the beneficial interests in a property are owned by a spouse in the main proceedings or the third party, or a combination of the two. If there is to be joinder, it is required to be dealt with in a structured manner, at an early stage, so that each party knows the case they have to meet. At paragraph 36 on *TL v ML*, Mostyn J said:

   [36] "In my opinion, it is essential in every instance where a dispute arises about the ownership of property in ancillary relief proceedings between a spouse and a third party, that the following things should ordinarily happen:

   (i) The third party should be joined to the proceedings at the earliest opportunity;

   (ii) Directions should be given for the issue to be fully pleaded by points of claim and points of defence;

   (iii) Separate witness statements should be directed in relation to the dispute; and

   (iv) The dispute should be directed to be heard separately as a preliminary issue, before the financial dispute resolution (FDR).

> *[37] "In this way, the parties will know at an early stage whether or not the property in question falls within the dispositive powers of the court and a meaningful FDR can take place. It also means that the expensive attendance of the third party for the entire duration of the trial can be avoided. It is a great pity that none of these steps took place in this case. Had they happened, I believe that a great deal of the costs would have been saved.*

6. That statement is a correct exposition of the law[2]. It is plainly helpful and indeed necessary for any intervenor to 'plead'[3] their case; and for the other parties to reply by way of a 'defence' or 'points of response'. That enables all parties to know the *basis* on which the third party is seeking to establish an interest, such as by way of an alleged common intention constructive trust[4], and for the third party to know whether that claim is accepted by the respondents or not, and if not, why not.

7. Notwithstanding the rule laid down by Mostyn J. in *TL v ML*, judges operating in the county courts in an era of budgetary austerity are frequently forced to make finely balanced case management decisions[5] when allocating valuable court resources to hearing such preliminary issues. Care must be taken to give trials of preliminary issues realistic estimates, for if they overrun then the FDR listed behind it will need to be vacated and re-listed, but with the parties now at the back of the FDR queue

2 Mostyn J.'s approach was commended by Munby J (as he then was) in *A v A* [2007] EWHC 99 (Fam) and by Thorpe LJ. in *Goldstone v Goldstone* [2011] 1 FLR 1926

3 In modern terminology namely to set out in a Statement of Case (called a Particulars of Claim if one is for the claimant in civil proceedings, but more usually called Points of Claim if one is an intervenor in family proceedings).

4 In TL v ML – the wife did not clearly set out her case. It was not until trial that her counsel clarified what type of trust that she was alleging existed. (She lost.)

5 This is a polite way of saying: occasionally unsatisfactory decisions.

again. Heaven forbid if the husband and wife fail to settle at the eventual FDR and then have to join the queue (once again) for a final hearing. The potential for delay and increased costs in a financial remedy claim involving TOLATA intervenors should certainly be borne in mind by the practitioner.[6] It is strongly suggested that time estimates for trials of preliminary issues, including time for reading and judgment, are realistic.

Costs consequences in trials of preliminary issues

8. The costs in a trial of a preliminary issue involving an intervenor in financial remedy proceedings are generally understood to be subject to the "clean sheet approach", per *Judge v Judge* [2009] 1 FLR 1287 and *Baker v Rowe* [2010] 1 FLR 761. That is because they are classified as 'family proceedings', meaning that CPR 44.2(2)[7] does not apply.[8] The clean sheet approach is different from the general rule in financial remedy proceedings that the court will make not make an order requiring one party to pay the costs of another party, as found in FPR 28.3(5). The clean sheet approach means that the Court can certainly make an order that costs follow the event, although that is not the formal starting point and it is not obligated to do so. That said, in Gojkovic (No 2)[9], Butler Sloss L.J. held that there remains the necessity for a starting point, and in her view it was that costs prima facie follow the event. This fits with subsequent reported examples of costs orders being made against unsuccessful parties in intervenor claims in financial remedy proceedings[10]. The wise

6 It is respectfully suggested that arbitration might be a more convenient mechanism for adjudicating on such disputes in many cases.

7 Namely, the general rule that the unsuccessful party will be ordered to pay the costs of the successful party.

8 CPR 44.2(2) is specifically disapplied from Part 28 (Costs) of the FPR by FPR 28.2(1).

9 [1992] Fam. 40, Court of Appeal, at 57.

10 Such as *A v A (No 2) (Ancillary Relief: Costs)* [2008] 1 FLR 1428, Munby J., and *KSO v MJO and JMO (PSO Intervening)* [2009] 1 FLR 1036,

practitioner will make it clear to his or her client that if they pursue, or defend, a weak or otherwise unmeritorious claim either as or against the third party, there is every chance that they may find themselves on the receiving end of a costs order, including potentially indemnity costs.[11]

9. On which party lies the duty to join a third party? The answer will differ from case to case. First, a third party has an "undoubted right to apply to intervene", per Mostyn J in *Fisher Meredith v JH and PH*[12]. But if the third party chooses not to, on which of the spouses is the duty incumbent? In the *Fisher Meredith* case, shares had been in the husband's legal name but which the husband had transferred to his aunt shortly before the proceedings began. The husband asserted that he had always held the shares as a bare trustee for his uncle, and was in effect giving them back (but to his uncle's wife). The aunt, incidentally, said she did not know why the husband had transferred them to her. The question was whether it was for the wife or the husband to join the aunt? Absolving the wife's solicitors of a first instance decision of professional negligence and a wasted costs order for not having joined the aunt, Mostyn J. held the duty to join the aunt was by no means clear cut. It may depend on whether one spouse (in that case, the wife) seeks an order which binds the third party for the purposes of enforcement.[13] In the instant case, Mostyn J held that, if anyone was at fault for

---

Munby J. again.

11 It has been held that the court has a wide discretion to award indemnity costs, and the test is whether the claim was unreasonably brought, rather than a test of moral condemnation. Where a claim is speculative, weak, opportunistic or thin, a claimant who chooses to pursue it takes a high risk and can expect to pay indemnity costs if it fails, per Tomlinson J in *Three Rivers District Council and Others v The Governor and Company of the Bank of England* [2006] EWHC 816.

12 [2012] 2 FLR 536 at para 50.

13 See paragraphs [50] to [52] of Mostyn J.'s judgment and his discussion of 'Pool A' and 'Pool B' cases.

not joining the husband's aunt, it was the husband. However, in a more typical case, where an applicant (let us call her the wife) says that property held in the name of a third party is the property of a respondent (let us call him the husband) then the burden of joinder falls upon the claimant wife, per Mostyn J at [43].

Interplay between TOLATA cases and Schedule 1 Children Act 1989 cases

10. It is increasingly common to see proceedings under Schedule 1 of the Children Act 1989, or the threat of the same, arising in a dispute under TOLATA 1996.

11. The most common example of this is where one party seeks an order for sale of jointly owned property, and the other, who has remained at the property, seeks to keep it until the parties' child has reach majority[14]. Reported cases however tend to only involve the super wealthy. There is very little guidance on the court's approach in more typical 'every day' cases. One reported example of a fairly typical case is *W v W* [2004] 2 FLR 321, which concerned the timing of an order for sale under TOLATA 1996. In that case, there was a formerly cohabiting couple with a single property between them. They had two children aged thirteen and eleven. The Mother, expecting that she would become the primary carer for the children, sought an order under TOLATA formally deferring the realisation of the Father's half share in the property until after the children's eighteenth birthdays. The Father applied for an immediate order for sale. In a perhaps ironic turn of events, the father was then awarded primary care of the children, the mother was not, and each parent then *reversed* their previous TOLATA positions. The Father thereafter sought to *keep* the property while

14 The practitioner should have regard to Schedule 1 of the Children Act, Paragraph 1, at sub-section (d) and (e), which permit the settling of property until a child is eighteen years old

the mother then sought to *sell* it. In the end, the trial judge *did* order a sale of the property. The judgment was described as far from perfect, but it was not overruled on appeal. Indeed, it appeared that in reaching his conclusion – although the information about the judgment before the Court of Appeal was limited – the trial judge had concluded that the children could be satisfactorily rehoused in a smaller, purchased property, based on the comparative property particulars in that case.

12. *W v W* demonstrates that such cases have fine margins. It is quite conceivable that one judge exercising his discretion may order a sale, and another may not. It is also quite normal for one party to claim under TOLATA to sell (or defer a sale of) a property, and for the other party to challenge this either under S.15 TOLATA in its own right, or additionally by bringing a cross Schedule 1 application to retain a property until the children reach eighteen, or in some cases, finish tertiary education.

13. How should any cross application under Schedule 1 be dealt with? *W v W* is again of assistance. In that case, Thorpe LJ noted, at paragraph 5, that:

> *"... As a matter of sensible management in the county court, if one co-owner invokes one statutory power and the other invokes a different statutory power, sensible management demands that the competing applications be conjoined. If one had to be given leading status, I would have myself assumed that it would be the application under Schedule 1, since that statute confers upon the court a much more extensive power, namely the power to make adjustive orders between the co-owners."*

14. Please note the language used by the learned judge, however. 'Conjoined' may of course mean "heard together" rather than formally "consolidated" under one case number. The rules and cost consequences relating to family and civil disputes are dif-

ferent. Moreover, finding a judge who can sit with both a civil and a family ticket can prove difficult in practice, particularly in the more complex cases.[15]

15. Finally concerning *W v W*, it is worth noting that in that case there was no dispute about the parties' beneficial interests. They both claimed a 50/50 share and therefore the real issue was the timing of the sale. It is more difficult to assess the interplay between Schedule 1 of the Children Act 1989 and TOLATA interplay when the quantum of the parties' beneficial interests are disputed.[16] In *N v D* [2008] 1 FLR 1629, a district judge of the Principal Registry of the Family Division made an order under Schedule 1 of the Children Act requiring a father to pay, inter alia, a lump sum to repair, renovate and enhance a property which housed his child and the mother, but in which he had the deferred beneficial interest (at page 1643).

15 Hence the rise in the popularity of arbitration. It is also to be hoped that the position may be alleviated by the trial at the time of writing of a specialist Financial Remedies Court system, sitting as part of the Single Family Court, as set out in Munby P.'s (as he then was) 'View from the President's Chamber' dated 23 January 2018. The idea is to have regional hubs overseen by specialist financial remedy practitioners. But importantly in this context, the then President added that the work of the FRC would extend "*in due course, [to] claims under the Inheritance (Provision for Family and Dependants) Act 1975 and claims under the Trusts of Land and Appointment of Trustees Act 1996 (TOLATA)*". Schedule 1 applications would be heard from the outset.

16 At the time of writing, there are no known reported examples of a consolidated case where a declaratory exercise was carried out under TOLATA, only to be interfered with by the application of Schedule 1, other than to create a child trust. Many such cases are prone to settlement.

Part II: An overview of civil procedure in TOLATA claims

A Part 7 or a Part 8 claim?

16. Freestanding TOLATA claims are brought under the Civil Procedure Rules 1998. Such cases may be brought under Part 7 or Part 8, depending on the nature of the case, as follows.

17. Part 7 proceedings are commenced in the typical civil litigation fashion, with a claim form and particulars of claim. They are most commonly used in a 'sole names' TOLATA case where one party is seeking to establish a beneficial share in a property of which the legal title is held by the other, or where one party is contending that there has been a change of intentions, which the other party does not accept has occurred. The normal requirements of CPR Part 15 and 16 (Defence and Reply; rules about statements of case) apply to Part 7 claims. It is worth noting, however, that there cannot be default judgment in a contentious TOLATA claim under CPR Part 12. If, for example, the claimant is seeking a beneficial share of the property in a sole name case, and the Defendant does not file his or her defence in time, the Court will not enter default judgment. That is because the claim is not be for a monetary sum, but rather is for declaratory relief. It is a judicial decision whether or not to grant declaratory relief, hence a court officer cannot grant a default judgment. A hearing will therefore be needed before a judge, even where the Defendant has not responded to the claim. To expedite matters, one could consider applying for summary judgment to take place at the first directions hearing to press the issue. One helpful corollary of the nature of such an application, is that claims for declaratory relief tend to attract a much lower Court issue fee than monetary claims (which are percentage based of the sum claimed, up to a cap). At the time of writing, the court fee for declaratory relief is £355, and many court offices accept this fee in such claims.

18. Part 8 claims are also frequently used. They are suited to joint names cases where there is no substantial dispute of fact as to the shares in which the parties hold the property and perhaps the only issues are likely to be whether and when a property should be sold, and/or the taking of an account.[17] A Part 8 claim begins with a short claim form with a witness statement in support. Note that in a Part 8 claim, the witness statement needs to be prepared at the outset of proceedings (including any exhibits such as bank and/or mortgage statements).

19. Part 8 does not contain the staggered process, seen in Part 7, where there are first statements of case or 'pleadings', then disclosure, and *then* the filing of witness evidence, often with one or more directions hearings in between. The case is front-loaded and ordinarily the claimant will get one chance and one chance only to file their witness evidence (including that of any witnesses), unless the court is persuaded otherwise[18]. A claimant may, however, file evidence in response to the Defendant's witness evidence.

20. Part 8 claims are not suited to claims where the beneficial interests are in dispute, and those should be properly pleaded under Part 7. Claims which are wrongly started under Part 8 are liable to be reallocated to Part 7 at the first directions hearing or case management conference.[19] Prejudice caused to the other

---

17 As to which, see Chapter 5.

18 CPR 8.6(1)(b)

19 One particular difficulty is what to do if one's client is served with a (misconceived) Part 8 Claim which should have been brought under Part 7. Whilst one can file an acknowledgment of service indicating that the Part 7 Procedure should have been used [Form N210, Box D], there may still be a dilemma as to whether to file a witness statement as required by the Part 8 rules – without prejudice to the contention that Part 8 has been wrongly invoked – or to take the risk of not doing so by keeping one's powder dry until the court has (hopefully) reallocated the case to Part 7, and pleadings and disclosure have been forthcoming.

party by starting under the wrong Part may well result in cost consequences.

21. In all TOLATA cases, an in-depth consideration of the issues is essential to start the case on the right foot (and indeed, on the right procedural track). Even under Part 7, where amendment of a statement of case is possible, there are cost and credibility consequences for doing so. The risks of being imprecise can be severe.

Costs case management

22. Practitioners should also beware of the likelihood of costs case management in TOLATA hearings. Costs case management applies to all Part 7 multi-track trials.[20] In such claims, unless the court otherwise orders, all parties except litigants in person must file and exchange budgets (a) where the stated value of the claim on the claim form is less than £50,000, with their directions questionnaires; or (b) in any other case, not later than 21 days before the first case management conference.[21]

23. If costs budgets cannot be agreed, there may be a costs and case management hearing to determine the proposed costs. For those who have never had the pleasure, undertaking a costs case management hearing is a bit like doing a 'summary assessment' of costs, but 'in anticipation' of the main event. At this pre-trial stage, the parties will file costs budgets[22] and if they cannot agree the predicted costs as being reasonable the court will assess those

20 The literal reading of CPR 3.12(1) is that the section relating to costs case management applies only to Part 7 multi-track hearings, and Part 8 is not included by omission. However, it has not been unknown for the courts in Part 8 claims to list costs and case management hearings in any event, so the practitioner is advised to check the notice of hearing carefully, to avoid falling foul of the rule to file a costs budget at least 21 days before a case management conference (CPR 3.13(1)(b))

21 CPR 3.13(1).

predicted costs at a hearing and cap as it sees fit the costs for some or all aspects of the future work on the case.[23]

Costs generally

24. TOLATA claims brought under the Civil Procedure Rules are subject to the normal costs consequences set out in Part 44 of those rules, and that means that, ordinarily, costs will follow the event, although the court may make a different order[24] That applies equally between Part 7 and Part 8 claims.

Part 36 Offers

25. Part 36 offers may of course be made in TOLATA claims. Two immediate points should be made by way of introduction. First, Part 36 of the Civil Procedure Rules forms its own, discrete, procedural code[25] and offers made within that section are not contractual in nature[26]. Secondly, Part 36 has evolved substantially since its inception in 1998 and was the subject of a very thorough revision in 2015. The case law on this part of the rules is substantial, and the practitioner is well advised to use a more

---

22 Which, after the event at a costs hearing, would be in the form of a costs schedule, but at this stage it is set out in a different form, Precedent H.

23 One of the unintended consequences of the Jackson reforms, which introduced costs budgeting, was the understandable concern of legal professionals that they would be strictly held to their approved budgets. Hence a tendency has arisen in practice for costs budgets to cover every possible contingency (such as an emergency application for further directions, or to put questions to an expert, or to apply for relief from sanctions); and also for practitioners to 'guess high' when estimating their costs, as they know that they can always come in under budget but must not go over budget.

24 CPR Rule 44.2(2).

25 CPR 36.1(1).

26 See *Flynn v Scougall* [2004] EWCA Civ 873.

detailed, costs-specific work, or the *White Book*[27] for further guidance.

26. As a general overview, some important points to remember may be summarised as follows (with the rule giving effect to the point in brackets):

Form

A Part 36 offer must[28]:

- be in writing;
- make clear that it is made pursuant to Part 36;
- specify a period of not less than 21 days within which the defendant will be liable for the claimant's costs in accordance with rule 36.13 or 36.20 if the offer is accepted;
- state whether it relates to the whole of the claim or to part of it or to an issue that arises in it and if so to which part or issue; and state whether it takes into account any counterclaim (*all per CPR 36.5)*
- It cannot, of course, be disclosed to a trial judge until after judgment has been given and the question of costs arises (*per CPR 36.16).*

27 Sweet & Maxwell.

28 Much progress has been made by the relatively recent introduction of Form N242A, which is designed to help eradicate mistakes of form which frequently arose owing to the technical nature of the rules. The Form is available on https://www.gov.uk/government/publications/form-n242a-notice-of-offer-to-settle-section-1-part-36

Who may make a Part 36 offer?

- Either party may make a Part 36 offer, although the cost consequences are different (*CPR 36.6 in conjunction with CPR 36.17*).

When can a Part 36 offer be made?

- A Part 36 offer may be made at any time, including before the commencement of proceedings (*per CPR 36.7(1)).*
- A Part 36 offer is made when it is served on the offeree (*per CPR 36.7(2)).*

Anything else?

- A request for clarification can be made on a Part 36 offer (per CPR 36.8).
- A Part 36 offer can be withdrawn, or have its terms changed, so long has the offeree has not yet served a notice of acceptance (per CPR 36.9(1)).
- A Part 36 offer can be written so that the offer may be automatically withdrawn after a period of time, provided it says so in its terms in accordance with its terms (per CPR 36.9(4)(b)).

And if the offer is accepted?

- As a general rule where a Part 36 offer is accepted within the relevant period the claimant will be entitled to the costs of the proceedings (including their recoverable pre-action costs) up to the date on which notice of acceptance was served on the offeror, per CPR 36.13(1), but this rule is subject to CPR 36.13 (2) –

namely an offer in relation to part of a claim only – and (4) (namely an offer made less than 21 days before trial or an offer accepted after the relevant period has expired).

- Costs will be assessed on the standard basis if not agreed, per CPR 36.13(3).
- Also, the claim will be stayed if an offer is accepted, per CPR 36.14(1).

And if the offer is not accepted, and if other side fails to better it?

- It depends on who wins.
- If the judgment against a defendant is at least as advantageous to the claimant as the proposals contained in a Claimant's Part 36 offer, then the cost consequences set out in Rule 36.17(4) shall apply, unless the court considers it unjust to do so. That rule provides that the claimant is entitled to—
    - interest on the whole or part of any sum of money (excluding interest) awarded, at a rate not exceeding 10% above base rate for some or all of the period starting with the date on which the relevant period expired;
    - costs (including any recoverable pre-action costs) on the indemnity basis from the date on which the relevant period expired;
    - interest on those costs at a rate not exceeding 10% above base rate; and
    - provided that the case has been decided and there has not been a previous order under this sub-para-

graph, an additional amount, which shall not exceed £75,000, calculated by applying the prescribed percentage set out below to an amount which is—

- o the sum awarded to the claimant by the court; or
- o where there is no monetary award, the sum awarded to the claimant by the court in respect of costs—

Amount awarded by the court	**Prescribed percentage**
Up to £500,000	10% of the amount awarded
Above £500,000	10% of the first £500,000 and (subject to the limit of £75,000) 5% of any amount above that figure.

- If, so far as the *Defendant* is concerned, the claimant fails to obtain a judgment more advantageous than the defendant's Part 36 offer, then CPR 36.17(3) shall apply, which provides that the Court must, unless it considers it unjust to do so, order that the defendant is entitled to:
  - o costs (including any recoverable pre-action costs) from the date on which the relevant period expired; and
  - o interest on those costs.
- It is therefore worth noting that the advantages to a Defendant of beating a Defendant's Part 36 offer are not are dramatic as a Claimant's beating of their offer. The costs are likely to be assessed on the standard basis

(because the rule does not provide that they shall be on the indemnity basis, although the Court may make a different order.

Does the Court have any wiggle room?

- Yes. As aforesaid it may not order the said cost consequences if it would be 'unjust' to do so. However, the discretion is limited. First, the Court must have regard to all the circumstances of the case including the factors set out in CPR 36.17(5), namely:
    - the terms of any Part 36 offer;
    - the stage in the proceedings when any Part 36 offer was made, including in particular how long before the trial started the offer was made;
    - the information available to the parties at the time when the Part 36 offer was made;
    - the conduct of the parties with regard to the giving of or refusal to give information for the purposes of enabling the offer to be made or evaluated; and;
    - whether the offer was a genuine attempt to settle the proceedings.
- Further, it has been held that "It is elementary that a judge who is asked to depart from the norm, on the ground that it would be 'unjust' not to do so, should not be tempted to make an exception merely because he or she thinks the regime itself harsh or unjust. There must be something about the particular circumstances of the case which takes it out of the norm", per *Downing v Peterborough & Stamford Hospitals NHS Foundation*

Trust [2015] 2 Costs L.O. 203, Sir David Eady, at para.61:

<u>What if the Part 36 offer was withdrawn at an earlier stage?</u>

- Then the cost consequences no longer apply, per CPR 36.17(7).

MORE BOOKS BY LAW BRIEF PUBLISHING

A selection of our other titles available now:-

'A Practical Guide to the SRA Principles, Individual and Law Firm Codes of Conduct 2019 – What Every Law Firm Needs to Know' by Paul Bennett
'A Practical Guide to Licensing Law for Commercial Property Lawyers' by Niall McCann & Richard Williams
'A Practical Guide to Adoption for Family Lawyers' by Graham Pegg
'Essential Motor Finance Law for the Busy Practitioner' by Richard Humphreys
'A Practical Guide to Industrial Disease Claims' by Andrew Mckie & Ian Skeate
'Employment Law and the Gig Economy' by Nigel Mackay & Annie Powell
'A Practical Guide to the Law of Armed Conflict' by Jo Morris & Libby Anderson
'A Practical Guide to Redundancy' by Philip Hyland
'A Practical Guide to Vicarious Liability' by Mariel Irvine
'A Practical Guide to Claims Arising from Delays in Diagnosing Cancer' by Bella Webb
'A Practical Guide to Applications for Landlord's Consent and Variation of Leases' by Mark Shelton
'A Practical Guide to Relief from Sanctions Post-Mitchell and Denton' by Peter Causton
'Butler's Equine Tax Planning: 2nd Edition' by Julie Butler
'A Practical Guide to Equity Release for Advisors' by Paul Sams
'A Practical Guide to Immigration Law and Tier 1 Entrepreneur Applications' by Sarah Pinder
'A Practical Guide to Unlawful Eviction and Harassment' by Stephanie Lovegrove
'In My Backyard! A Practical Guide to Neighbourhood Plans' by Dr Sue Chadwick
'A Practical Guide to the Law Relating to Food' by Ian Thomas

'A Practical Guide to the Ending of Assured Shorthold Tenancies' by Elizabeth Dwomoh
'Commercial Mediation – A Practical Guide' by Nick Carr
'A Practical Guide to Financial Services Claims' by Chris Hegarty
'The Law of Houses in Multiple Occupation: A Practical Guide to HMO Proceedings' by Julian Hunt
'A Practical Guide to Unlawful Eviction and Harassment' by Stephanie Lovegrove
'A Practical Guide to Solicitor and Client Costs' by Robin Dunne
'Artificial Intelligence – The Practical Legal Issues' by John Buyers
'A Practical Guide to Wrongful Conception, Wrongful Birth and Wrongful Life Claims' by Rebecca Greenstreet
'Occupiers, Highways and Defective Premises Claims: A Practical Guide Post-Jackson – 2nd Edition' by Andrew Mckie
'A Practical Guide to Financial Ombudsman Service Claims' by Adam Temple & Robert Scrivenor
'A Practical Guide to the Law of Enfranchisement and Lease Extension' by Paul Sams
'A Practical Guide to Marketing for Lawyers – 2nd Edition' by Catherine Bailey & Jennet Ingram
'A Practical Guide to Advising Schools on Employment Law' by Jonathan Holden
'Certificates of Lawful Use and Development: A Guide to Making and Determining Applications' by Bob Mc Geady & Meyric Lewis
'A Practical Guide to the Law of Dilapidations' by Mark Shelton
'A Practical Guide to the 2018 Jackson Personal Injury and Costs Reforms' by Andrew Mckie
'A Guide to Consent in Clinical Negligence Post-Montgomery' by Lauren Sutherland QC
'A Practical Guide to Running Housing Disrepair and Cavity Wall Claims: 2nd Edition' by Andrew Mckie & Ian Skeate
'A Practical Guide to the General Data Protection Regulation (GDPR)' by Keith Markham
'A Practical Guide to Digital and Social Media Law for Lawyers' by Sherree Westell

'A Practical Guide to Holiday Sickness Claims – 2nd Edition'
by Andrew Mckie & Ian Skeate

'A Practical Guide to Inheritance Act Claims by Adult Children Post-Ilott v Blue Cross' by Sheila Hamilton Macdonald

'A Practical Guide to Elderly Law' by Justin Patten

'Arguments and Tactics for Personal Injury and Clinical Negligence Claims'
by Dorian Williams

'A Practical Guide to QOCS and Fundamental Dishonesty' by James Bentley

'A Practical Guide to Drone Law' by Rufus Ballaster, Andrew Firman, Eleanor Clot

'Practical Mediation: A Guide for Mediators, Advocates, Advisers, Lawyers, and Students in Civil, Commercial, Business, Property, Workplace, and Employment Cases' by Jonathan Dingle with John Sephton

'Practical Horse Law: A Guide for Owners and Riders' by Brenda Gilligan

'A Comparative Guide to Standard Form Construction and Engineering Contracts'
by Jon Close

'A Practical Guide to Compliance for Personal Injury Firms Working With Claims Management Companies' by Paul Bennett

'A Practical Guide to the Landlord and Tenant Act 1954: Commercial Tenancies'
by Richard Hayes & David Sawtell

'A Practical Guide to Personal Injury Claims Involving Animals' by Jonathan Hand

'A Practical Guide to Psychiatric Claims in Personal Injury' by Liam Ryan

'Introduction to the Law of Community Care in England and Wales'
by Alan Robinson

'A Practical Guide to Dog Law for Owners and Others' by Andrea Pitt

'Ellis and Kevan on Credit Hire – 5th Edition' by Aidan Ellis & Tim Kevan

'RTA Allegations of Fraud in a Post-Jackson Era: The Handbook – 2nd Edition'
by Andrew Mckie

'RTA Personal Injury Claims: A Practical Guide Post-Jackson' by Andrew Mckie

'On Experts: CPR35 for Lawyers and Experts' by David Boyle

'An Introduction to Personal Injury Law' by David Boyle

'A Practical Guide to Claims Arising From Accidents Abroad and Travel Claims'
by Andrew Mckie & Ian Skeate

'A Practical Guide to Cosmetic Surgery Claims' by Dr Victoria Handley
'A Practical Guide to Chronic Pain Claims' by Pankaj Madan
'A Practical Guide to Claims Arising from Fatal Accidents' by James Patience
'A Practical Approach to Clinical Negligence Post-Jackson' by Geoffrey Simpson-Scott
'A Practical Guide to Personal Injury Trusts' by Alan Robinson
'Employers' Liability Claims: A Practical Guide Post-Jackson' by Andrew Mckie
'A Practical Guide to Subtle Brain Injury Claims' by Pankaj Madan
'The Law of Driverless Cars: An Introduction' by Alex Glassbrook
'A Practical Guide to Costs in Personal Injury Cases' by Matthew Hoe
'A Practical Guide to Alternative Dispute Resolution in Personal Injury Claims – Getting the Most Out of ADR Post-Jackson' by Peter Causton, Nichola Evans, James Arrowsmith
'A Practical Guide to Personal Injuries in Sport' by Adam Walker & Patricia Leonard
'The No Nonsense Solicitors' Practice: A Guide To Running Your Firm' by Bettina Brueggemann
'Baby Steps: A Guide to Maternity Leave and Maternity Pay' by Leah Waller
'The Queen's Counsel Lawyer's Omnibus: 20 Years of Cartoons from The Times 1993-2013' by Alex Steuart Williams

These books and more are available to order online direct from the publisher at www.lawbriefpublishing.com, where you can also read free sample chapters. For any queries, contact us on 0844 587 2383 or mail@lawbriefpublishing.com.

Our books are also usually in stock at www.amazon.co.uk with free next day delivery for Prime members, and at good legal bookshops such as Wildy & Sons.

We are regularly launching new books in our series of practical day-to-day practitioners' guides. Visit our website and join our free newsletter to be kept informed and to receive special offers, free chapters, etc.

You can also follow us on Twitter at www.twitter.com/lawbriefpub.

www.ingramcontent.com/pod-product-compliance
Lightning Source LLC
LaVergne TN
LVHW052326200926
848481LV00002B/680